# BIOGRAPHICAL INFORMATION

Johann Wilhelm Heisman was born October 23, 1869, in Cleveland. His father, a maker and repairer of barrels, soon moved the family to Titusville, Pennsylvania, where the business prospered as a result of its proximity to the oil industry. John lived the majority of his young life in the area, until he enrolled at Brown in 1887. Heisman focused much of his time at Brown on athletics, especially baseball and the informal club football team. In 1887, he transferred to the University of Pennsylvania, where he studied law and first played in official intercollegiate football. Heisman earned a law degree from Penn in 1892, but due to an eye injury requiring him to rest his eyes for two years, he forewent the practice of law, accepting instead the position of head football coach at Oberlin College in Ohio.

Besides Oberlin, Heisman's thirty-six-year coaching career took him to Auburn, Clemson, Georgia Tech, Akron, Penn, Washington and Jefferson, and Rice. One of the winningest coaches in history, when he retired in 1927, after a three-decade-long coaching career, his overall record was 185 victories, 68 losses, and 18 ties. Among these victories was the most lopsided win in history, when his 1916 Georgia Tech team defeated Cumberland 222-0. Well known as a tactician, Heisman introduced many innovations to football and greatly facilitated its move into the modern era. Among other things, he originated the center snap, the hidden-ball play, the Heisman shift (forerunner of the T and I formations), and the scoreboard listing yardage, downs, and other essential information. Yet, probably his most important contribution to the game was his fight to legalize the forward pass, a maneuver which greatly opened up the game and lessened the number of injuries (and even deaths!) on the playing field. A strict disciplinarian with a no-loss attitude, he was particularly respected for his complete-player perspective focusing on both the physical and mental aspects of the game, coupled with stern leadership on how players (and coaches) should always be gentlemen.

When Heisman resigned from coaching in 1927, he moved to New York City, where he opened a sporting goods store and ran the Downtown Athletic Club (DAC). In 1935, he inaugurated the Downtown Athletic Club Trophy for the best college football player east of the Mississippi (the scope of the award was soon thereafter enlarged to include the entire nation). John Heisman died October 3, 1936, at the age of sixty-six. The DAC Trophy was awarded for the second time two months after his death, but it had since been renamed the Heisman Memorial Trophy. The trophy is given annually and remains the most prestigious honor awarded to individual players in college football.

# THE WISDOM OF JOHN HEISMAN

## ALWAYS

Always play with your head.
Always run your fastest.
Always tackle low.
Always be where the ball is.
Always win the game.

## DON'T

Don't try to play without your head.
Don't see how light you can hit, but how hard.
Don't stop running because you are behind.
Don't "blow"; keep calm, cool, and determined—but
    FIGHT all the way.
Don't lose the game.

## CAN'T

You can't make the team if you don't understand
    teamwork.
You can't do yourself justice without getting and
    staying in condition.
You can't afford to waste time talking.
You can't afford to loaf any during football season.
You can't win without knowing these principles.

## NEVER

Never get excited.
Never give up.
Never play less than your very hardest.
Never come on the field without your brain.
Never forget a football player may be a gentleman.

# PRINCIPLES OF FOOTBALL

# Principles of Football

by
JOHN HEISMAN

*WITH ILLUSTRATIONS*

HILL STREET PRESS d ATHENS, GEORGIA

A HILL STREET PRESS BOOK

Published in the United States of America by
Hill Street Press LLC    191 East Broad Street, Suite 209
Athens, Georgia 30601-2848 USA    706-613-7200
info@hillstreetpress.com    www.hillstreetpress.com

Sporting by its nature is potentially hazardous. The publisher does not assume any
liability for injury sustained while undertaking any of the activities recommended in
this book. All participants assume responsibility for their own actions and safety.

Hill Street Press books are available in bulk purchase and customized editions for
institutions and corporate accounts. Please contact us for more information.

Printed in Canada.

Library of Congress Cataloging-in-Publication Data

Heisman, John W. (John William), 1869–1936.
    Principles of football / John Heisman.
        p.    cm.
    Reprint. Originally published: St. Louis : Sports Pub. Bureau, ©1922.
    ISBN 1-892514-99-0 (alk. paper)
        1. Football. 2. Football players—Training of. I. Title.
    GV951 .H45 2000
    796.332'2–dc21                    00-059669

ISBN# 1-892514-99-0

10  9  8  7  6  5  4  3  2  1

First printing

# TABLE OF CONTENTS.

# FOREWORD

By no means is it claimed that this is an exhaustive treatment of the subject of Football. Neither is it designed to supplant or supersede existing publications of excellence and undoubted merit. It is merely the writer's contribution to the literature of the game.

Probably there is not a great deal inside these pages that coaches and the more experienced college players do not already know. For instance, it is not unlikely they are familiar with every formation and play to be found in the book. But my aim has not been to scatter a mass of "shot gun" information over a wide field. What I have tried to do was to correlate facts and state concrete principles, and to aid coaches and players by giving to these principles clear and direct pronouncement. To High and Preparatory School players, it is especially hoped, the work may prove useful by giving sound basic advice in language easily comprehended.

Take the chapter of Axioms. The author knows of no published work on the great college game that contains anything like this. Thus summarized the terse statement of these playing and coaching principles will, it is believed, be helpful as "Reminders" even to fairly experienced coaches. They are outlines of topics that should be presented for consideration by every football squad, at some stage or other of the season. For the past twenty years I have lectured from them to my squads and would, frankly, feel lost without them.

The Author.

# Principles of Football

## CHAPTER I.

### BENEFITS OF FOOTBALL.

The physical benefits of football playing, as
of every other good outdoor sport, have been
retailed so often I need not stop for them. But
their valuable mental and moral effects have
not yet, it seems to me, been set forth as they
deserve. I shall make a lame attempt.

It has always struck the writer as singular
that we have nowhere a school for the training
and strengthening of moral qualities of the
mind of our youth. Schools and colleges have
we in abundance wherein is imparted knowledge of almost every known art and science.
And if the boy's body needs training and education we can put him through gymnasiums or
out on the cinder track and, under readily
accessible trained supervision, his muscles are
toughened, his lungs enlarge, he becomes quick
and supple and what not.

Again, his spiritual needs are looked after
by trained theologians who officiate in mag-
nificent temples.

All very good—as far as it goes. But where

1

can the growing, developing young man get
training for moral qualities of mind, for his
psycho? Is there a school of any kind where a
boy's Will or Temper or Disposition can be
trained? Has any scientific study been put on
the question of how these mental qualities may
be strengthened? The writer knows of no such
institution.

But is it certain that a young man ought by all
means to have the proper development of his
will power looked after? The doctor regulates
his liver, the dentist looks after his teeth, the
college professor undertakes to give him his
all-essential dose of geometry, the gymnasium
instructor makes sure that his muscles become
firm and reliable—are these not enough? I
leave it to the reader to say whether it is or is
not a matter of importance that a young man
start out in life with an ability to shut his jaws
hard and say "I will," or "I will not," and
mean it.

## Will Power.

If it is conceded that the development of
a dependable will in every young man is not
only worth while, but is actually indispensable,
then I can tell you that the athletic field is
about the best laboratory known where the
young man can get the training, the discipline,
the experience that will systematically and
inevitably turn the trick. And football is the
game that will build up will power in a boy's

immature mind just about five times faster than anything else in this world.

## Self Control.

To learn to hold one's temper is a great achievement. This accomplishment is not taught in our college class-rooms. It is occasionally talked of in Sunday School. But the average boy seldom gets a practical chance to try himself out on the subject save through the medium of participation in athletic games and sports. And of these by far the best for the purpose is football. Your footballer is compelled to control himself, though the game, with its man to man contacts, is the one above all others in which his good nature and serenity of disposition are tried often and long. It's worth playing the game to acquire this splendid self control.

## Clear Thinking.

Ability to think rapidly and correctly under fire. Any place save the athletic field where we teach boys how to do that? Not that I know of. We preach to them, yes—but do we teach them? Examinations, it might be claimed, do this. Yes, they compel the boy to think, and there is considerable importance hinging on his thinking correctly. But as a rule he has plenty of time in which to do the thinking when endeavoring to pass an examination. And the circumstances and conditions surrounding a scholastic examination are not exciting in the least. It is no such case of being "under fire" as is presented by the man to man shock of a football game in a surcharged atmosphere. Consider, there never lived a boy who was not wildly, madly excited on going into his first game. But in time he learns to keep cool and to think calmly and clearly in the very thick of the most exciting and nerve tingling episodes; and he comes to correct conclusions, he makes flawless decisions in the fraction of a second time and time again in the course of every five minutes on the gridiron.

Isn't that something worth while? Where else can you give him not merely wordy advice on such a subject, but actual practice? Not in the school room and not in the Church; so much am I sure of.

### Memory.

And then it trains a boy's memory. He has to learn complicated and puzzling signals, and to remember just what they mean. And he must recall what his duty is under that mysterious command and how it is to be performed.

Yes, he does also have to remember things expounded by and from his text books. But as he cares more for football than for studies, he strives harder to remember what the coach tells him. If so be he has a poor memory and disappoints by slow development in the classroom, it's a lucky thing for him that he can have the chance to strengthen that poor memory by earnest participation in the great game of football.

## Scholastic Standing.

At most schools and colleges a boy is not permitted to play if he begins to fall down in his classroom work. This is as it should be, for, primarily, the youth goes to college to get a mental education. Well, many a boy that doesn't care particularly for studies has been pulled through by this very rule; he is so fond of football that he actually makes up his mind to get down to business in his studies in order that he may continue with football. Behold the game has made the boy a student. Is not that to the credit of the game?

## Sportsmanship.

In no game and in no calling is there so strong a temptation for a participant to cheat, to take unfair advantages, to do small, petty, mean things, to lose temper, to indulge in profanity, to quarrel, to show a nasty disposition, and even to resort to downright fighting, as in football.

Better stay away from such a pastime, say you? Not I! That's the time, the place and the way to learn how to govern, to control, to conquer yourself. On properly regulated fields you see even the coaches frowning such things down. The up-to-date coach will no longer encourage nor even permit "dirty" playing or muckerism of any kind by any of his players. And it is in the game to make the participants admire even an opponent who does big things in a big way. If a player is a real sportsman his example is contagious and the rest desire to emulate him. On a properly regulated field there is not place any longer even for profanity or for indecent language of any kind. Will not this help at least a little in the right moulding of a boy's character?

And now the game has made our hero a sportsman and a gentleman.

## The Formation of Good Habits.

On a properly organized team every man must conform absolutely to a very rigorous system of training. It is against the coach's rules to smoke, to chew tobacco, to drink liquor, to stay out late at night, to frequent improper resorts, to gamble, to bet on the games, to eat candy or to drink the ruinous messes that the average non-playing boy pours hourly into his stomach. His indulgence in cake, pie, pastry, and other foods of questionable value is kept at a minimum. He is obligated to study and to satisfy his teachers, because failure to do so not merely injures himself but jeopardizes the chances of the team and the hopes of the whole college.

Isn't this worth while to any boy? And would anything save love of the game make him willing to go through it all?

Take the matter of discipline: The football candidate learns to obey orders promptly, cheerfully, without question. Whether he likes the order or not, he has no choice but to obey unfalteringly and at once. Not willingly does he submit himself to such discipline anywhere else in his student sphere of life, but here he learns to toe the mark. Isn't it one of the very best things in the world for him?

Many other unthought of benefits come from a right participation in football, but I will speak of but one more.

We all know that by collegians the game is esteemed the king of sports, and it deserves no less ranking, for it has the power to create and to arouse "college spirit" as does nothing else from one end of the campus to another. Now college spirit is a mighty fine thing. It teaches the meaning of the words loyalty, fidelity, love of country, patriotism.

I wish to go further: Sometimes am I asked whether it is considered good form for the players to inform on each other in cases of infraction of the training rules. I reply that in any institution where football has reached a high stage of perfection and has become the dominant institution in undergraduate life, it is not only the correct thing for members of the team to report to the Head Coach any infractions of the training rules, but it is the bounden duty of any and every man in the entire college to so report anything of that sort.

No, boys will not report on one another the playing of college pranks and jokes; but breaking training is no prank and no joke. It is a breaking, in effect, of a man's word of honor. A member of the football team has others to whom he is answerable in his conduct besides himself. If he is derelict in his duty he harms others as well. He is liable to undo the whole season's work of the coaches, to nullify completely the herculean efforts that a hundred men have been making for months to turn out a flawless machine that shall bring fame and honor to themselves and undying glory to Alma Mater. More, he is risking blasting the high hopes and breaking the hearts of thousands of Alumni and undergraduates, of trustees, of faculty members, of friends and well-wishers throughout the length and breadth of the land. The man has been trained and labored with zealously and painstakingly for weeks to make him fit to hold down a certain responsible position. True, he is but a cog, but of what use in any machine is the rest of the wheel if even one cog slips. To break training without permission is nothing more nor less than an act of treason. If, against orders, a sentry strikes a match wherewith to light his pipe, thus exposing a position to the enemy, would it be the job of only his superior officers to report him or would it not be the patriotic duty of every comrade and of any private citizen to denounce him?

Well, that's the code that governs in a real football college, and it's the right one. The college publications support the Head Coach in such a drastic policy, likewise the fraternities, the clubs and classes. They would not be worthy of the happiness that comes from clean success if they did not stand by such a system. That's what co-operation is—**that's college spirit!**

## CHAPTER II.

## THE FOOTBALL COACH.

The position of a college football coach is unique. It is the rarest thing in the world for any man to become a successful coach of this game unless he has had plenty of high-grade playing experience in the game, and such experience he cannot get save with some college team. This means that he is all but invariably a college man, and that implies that he is usually a different type of man from the professional coach that never went to college, no matter what game or sport is his specialty.

Rightly or wrongly, professional coaches of games are often regarded as illiterate men, of little refinement of manner and uncouth in appearance—in short, "rough necks." But for a long time people have understood that the average modern football coach is a man of education and culture, occupying not only a prominent but an important position in the world of affairs. By this I do not refer to the newspaper notoriety he achieves, nor to the salary he may command, nor yet to the fact that, at a big game, he is the cynosure of all eyes and that his name is likely to be on a thousand lips at once. I mean he is an important personage in the sense that he is in a position, he has the undoubted power, to make or mar the lives and whole future careers of something like a hundred young men every year that he is in charge of football at this, that or the other institution.

That's a strong statement, but it won't miss the mark far. For 30 years the writer has been coaching college football teams, handling close to an average of a hundred collegians every fall. That experience has told me a lot about young men and football, especially regarding the result when the two are scrambled, and I make the deliberate statement that, in a majority of cases, a successful football coach can do more, either for good or for evil, with the average player of school and collegiate age than can any other person under the sun. The lad is "deaf to the voice of consanguinity," but he will do most anything short of committing murder for a winning coach.

Now this is what I term a unique position for a coach to occupy. It means that he has an extraordinary and dangerous power. Some coaches realize they have this power and some do not; but not all of the former sense what a tremendous responsibility devolves upon them.

Consider a moment: The coach can use his singular power to the greatest possible good for a young man or he can do him the worst kind of an injury. Whatever the coach says goes with the impressionable young pupil. The coach's word is the law and the gospel, and that not merely as regards football but as to most anything under the sun.

At that age a boy's mind is plastic. Certain things are much more apt to get control of his mind, his heart, his emotional nature than others. One of these is football, and through the medium of this wonderful game the coach, quite unintentionally, gets control of the boy. The coach says, "Do this!" and the boy does it, though his own father or mother might not have been able to get compliance.

And so it comes that that boy at just that time of life is likely to be taught things by the coach and to get into habits engendered and fostered by the way his coach acts and thinks that will stick to him for the remainder of his life.

If the coach is a worthless, reprehensible fellow, a man of bad character or none, he is bound to do the boys enormous harm. If, however, he is a high type of man with lofty ideals and firm principles of right and truth, one who recognizes his power and his responsibilities, then it's well he coaches football and it's well for the boys that play football under him that they went to that School. Such a man will do more downright character building for the boys than can nineteen ministers out of twenty, or ninety-nine fathers out of a hundred. Why?

Because he has the influence over them that counts at the impressionable age.

This is a matter that parents should ponder when they are about to send their sons to college, and a matter that all coaches should reflect on most seriously every day of their lives. More than parents, more than professors they have it in their power to make or break for all time the character of the young men under them.

## CHAPTER III.

### TRAINING FOR FOOTBALL.

Ambitious footballers understand that a systematic course of training is vital to success on the gridiron.

The teams of high grade are all handled by expert trainers who know their business. But the younger school players are, as a rule, not so blessed. For their benefit I will set down a few rules covering the more important matters of training—a strict observance of which will answer almost all purposes.

(1) A football player should not use tobacco in any form while the season is on.

(2) He should not partake of spirituous or alcoholic drinks of any kind.

(3) He should not drink soda waters containing artificial syrups. Drinks made of pure fruit juices like lemonade, orangeade, etc., are harmless.

(4) Ice cream, if pure, a couple of times a week is all right.

(5) Eat sparingly of pastry and rich desserts. No pie or cake or candy, no syrup or molasses.

Occasionally a plain dessert like bread, rice or tapioca pudding will pass muster.

(6) A player should do without coffee altogether during the season. Tea is not so bad. The staple drinks, of course, are water, sweet milk and buttermilk.

(7) Most any meats are good except fresh pork and veal. Beef, mutton, lamb, chicken and fish are all splendid, especially broiled or roasted. No fried meat of any kind should be eaten by an athlete.

(8) Nearly all vegetables get the stamp of approval except cabbage, which should not be eaten in any form.

(9) Potatoes are best when baked. Mashed and stewed potatoes will do—but never fried potatoes. In fact, fried vegetables of any kind should be as carefully avoided as fried meats. Rice, beans, peas, spinach, lettuce, parsnips carrots may all be freely eaten.

(10) All bread should either be stale or toasted; no hot bread of any kind.

(11) Most kinds of fruit are all right. Bananas that are the least bit green had better be left alone.

Dates and prunes are especially good and can be eaten to advantage in fairly large quantities.

All kinds of nuts are bad.

(12) Eggs poached, soft boiled or scrambled fill the bill nicely; never eat them fried.

(13) Most cereals are beneficial. Oat meal, cream of wheat and cracked wheat are fine. Shredded wheat will do. The others will pass but have not so much nutritive value. Mush and milk is fine.

(14) Food for a football player should never be highly seasoned and all condiments must be pretty generally side-stepped. I refer particularly to pepper, vinegar, mustard, catsup, horseradish and the like.

(15) Good butter can be used in generous quantities.

(16) Soups do no special harm but, contrary to general belief, there is very little nutrition in them.

(17) There should be little or no eating between meals, though if one is excessively hungry late at night a piece of bread and butter or a few crackers would do no special harm. An apple would be better.

(18) Meals should be eaten at regular hours. It is best to have a lunch at noon and dinner in the evening after the hard afternoon practice.

(19) Breakfast might consist of fruit, cereal, eggs, a chop and toast. Even a little crisp bacon wouldn't hurt once or twice a week, though not on the morning of the game. A steak is just as good as a chop.

(20) For lunch one might rest content with roast beef, hot or cold, baked potatoes, toast and tea, or milk.

(21) Dinner could nicely consist of steak, or chicken, or roast beef or fish, with potatoes, rice, stewed tomatoes, toast, tea and a plain pudding.

The last meal before a game should be simple indeed; somebody should see to it that none of the players eat a big hearty meal. Roast beef, mashed or baked potatoes, toast and tea or milk are quite enough.

A footballer should retire not later than 10:30 p. m., unless it is absolutely necessary for him to stay up a bit later for study. But in any event he must get at least eight hours sleep every night, undisturbed by noises or interruptions of any kind. The night before a game he should be in bed by 10:30 and should stay there until 7:30 the next morning.

In the early days of the fall campaign the players perspire very freely and can hardly get enough water to drink. For the first week or so they may be permitted to have almost as much as they want, but after that their allowance should be cut down while playing, for it is impossible to do brilliant athletic work with a stomach full of water. Accordingly, orders should be given that the water bucket is not to be brought on the field until called for by the Coach, who then sees to it that no man gets more than half of a small dipperful at a time. As soon as practice is over a player can drink as much as he wishes.

On Sundays all football men should take a long walk of four or five miles to work the stiffness out of their muscles from the previous day's game.

Contrary to some training rules, I do not consider it a good plan for players to be sent on a long two to four mile run every morning before breakfast. It is altogether too exhausting and drains too much of their vitality. They can get all the work they need in the regular two-hour afternoon practice.

## CHAPTER IV.

## HOW TO PLAY THE DIFFERENT POSITIONS.

### Center.

The Center on a football team must be a man who can think coolly, clearly and rapidly. Others can miss a signal now and then without great harm resulting—but not the center. He must never mistake to whom he is to snap the ball, nor the direction in which the runner is to travel. Should he "fall down" the whole play would go to pieces on the spot.

Having found a man that will do, so far as these mental qualifications go, we next inquire whether he knows how to snap the ball. Even if he has never had experience at this delicate task it is entirely possible to teach him satisfactorily in a week or two, provided he has a little talent, though there are some men who never can learn how a football should be snapped. They simply haven't the correct mental and physical co-ordination.

When a signal comes that calls for the ball to be snapped into action the ball must come back instantly. This does not mean that it must come with great momentum or immense velocity—not at all; but it must *start* on its backward flight without delay. For the same signal which called for the ball also shot all the players into action simultaneously, and unless the ball gets into action forthwith the men will be in motion ahead of the ball, and that will call for a penalty. It's like a sprinter on his mark— he must not only be a fast runner, once he gets started, but he must learn *how to start*.

Unlike the football, the sprinter can leap into action on the pistol shot to the very limit of his explosive ability and galvanize into top speed action as quickly as he likes. A football, however, must not travel at that top speed, no matter how soon after "the pistol" it starts; it must come gently even though immediately.

The ball should be snapped low—a bit above the knees—for a plunge into the line, and directly at the back that is to carry it. In other words you do not "lead" a bucker ever, whereas you do lead a runner when he is starting for an end run. How much do you lead for an end run? That all depends on how fast and how quickly the runner starts, how far back he is when he starts, whether it's a long end run or a short end run, and whether the ball is wet or dry.

Naturally, you can lead a quick starter and fast runner further than you can a man that starts slowly and has but little speed. The snapper has to learn the different starting and running speeds of his backs and must be governed accordingly. And the further back from the line the back starts, the further can you lead him. If, for instance, he is standing ten yards back on a punt formation and the signal calls for him to run around his own right end you could lead him two or three times as far to the right as you could if he were within four yards of the scrimmage line, for it will take a much longer time for the ball to travel back that far than if he stood at the closer distance, and in that longer interval he can run a much greater distance to the right to gather in the ball.

Do not lead the runner as far with a wet ball as you would with a dry ball.

For an end run the ball should be aimed, on close formation plays, at the lacing of a man's pants, while if he is back 10 yards it should be aimed at his chest, whether he is going to run or punt.

On punt formation it may well come back as a spiral; the sooner the punter gets it into his hands the more time he will have to adjust it and to look over the field and note how fast his line is getting down and how much he is about to be hurried by opponents. All those are matters of much importance to the punter. On shorter snaps the ball should always go back less swiftly—"floated" for an end run so it can easily be "picked out of the air," while for a buck it should be sent straighter and with only medium velocity, never slammed.

So we see that in correct snapping a center

should have regard for four things: (1) passing the ball instantly on the snapping signal; (2) giving it the proper velocity; (3) aiming it at the right height and for the correct distance, and (4) remembering what lead, if any, to give to each play and player.

To do these things well you must be well braced on your feet. Do not have them "on an even keel." They are not to be on the same line parallel to the scrimmage line, but spread well apart, and one behind the other, so that you are well braced in both directions—sideways and forward and back. Remember your opponent will probably crash into you the instant you have snapped the ball and you'll make a bad snap if you aren't properly braced. Neither leg should be fully straightened out. You must have something of the set of the sprinter—both knees flexed a little, so you can yourself get a quick charge, either to help open up if the play is to come through center, or else to go through quickly and get a man in the secondary defense.

Be careful not to let your elbows strike the insides of your thighs as you swing your arms back with the ball, else the ball won't go through to the target. Carry your arms clear through on their swing so as to guide the ball as long as possible on its backward flight.

On charging keep your feet till you get to your man, then leave them and dive with your body crosswise just at his knees, so as to cut out his legs from under him. You should have a pretty good idea of just where your man is playing or where you expect to find him before ever you snap the ball. Study him all the time.

When it comes to defense your duties are equally important.

Most teams frequently play the center back of the line a yard or two instead of up in the rush line. In such a defensive system he is referred to as the "loose" or "roving" center. His duty is to back up the whole line from one end to the other.

When the opposing runner starts through, the center is expected to be right on the spot to nail him or to take first crack at him. This means that the center must be a deadly tackler —a fearless, aggressive, tireless player and one who never knows the meaning of the word surrender; a man whose play all over the field should be an inspiration to his teammates. Such a center is in the best possible position to diagnose his opponents' formation and plays, and he is expected to advise his comrades as to his idea of what is coming; he may be given supreme authority on the defense to place or set the entire eleven.

In addition he will have to be made use of all the time to help break up forward passes. He should sense when they are about to come off and must have initiative to move in the correct direction. He should be quick to cover ground, and he should be fairly tall so as to be able to reach up in the air and dispute possesssion of any forward pass.  Basketball experience would be very helpful to a roving center.

This man should weigh, on a college team of fair weight, about 175 pounds and be close to six feet tall; height will enable him to look over into the opponents' backyard, which is an advantage when it comes to diagnosing the play.

While still generally called the center, this player is more properly denominated the snapper, for, in a majority of cases nowadays, the man who snaps the ball in scrimmage is by no means the center man of the rush line.  There are so many unbalanced formations that, in the writer's opinion, "snapper" would be a better name for him.

The position is a grand one to play and excellence therein does not seem to positively demand men of any special weight or size. Schultz, of Michigan, and Torrey, of Pennsylvania, rank among the greatest centers of all time.  Schultz weighed 250 whereas Torrey beamed only 160.

### Guard.

The position of guard on a football team is usually regarded as prosaic and unattractive. That's partly because a guard never runs with the ball and partly because he is usually instructed to remain in defensive position to stop assaults aimed directly at his location.  This last means that he is merely the under dog in a badly messed-up situation, for attacks at guards are usually of a mass nature and do not often offer him opportunities for clean and brilliant-looking tackles such as centers or ends or halves can make in the open field.

And yet two of the very greatest half dozen players the game has ever produced were guards—Hefflefinger, of Yale, and Hare, of Pennsylvania. And other wonderful players were guards, such as Brown, of Yale, Felton, of Harvard, DeWitt, of Princeton, and Wharton, of Pennsylvania. This shows it is not so much the position that makes a player loom up but rather the kind of player that is occupying that position.

To stand the gruelling work of guard tip-top physique is required. A guard should be heavy and very strong. If he can be tall and rangy— as were all the men whose names I have mentioned—so much the better. They must have splendid endurance and mental doggedness. On defense the sameness of their work may make things grow very monotonous, but they must be chaps who can stick to their guns and know what it is to "die in the last ditch" with never a thought of yielding a single inch.

On the offense a guard may, by the rules, interlock his feet with those of the snapper if he wishes. This alone shows how close a guard is expected to play to the snapper. In other words "tight line" is the rule here as nowhere else on the scrimmage line. The backs must be absolutely unmolested in their own backyard till they can get started. Nothing is so calculated to throw them into confusion as to have an opposing guard or center come knifing through on them before the play is well started. To obviate this danger the guards should never grow so careless as to line up loosely or with gaps between them and the snapper.

Also a guard must be thoughtful about how and where he puts his feet. Bad snaps are often caused by a guard having one or other of his feet directly in the way of the snap back. As a rule he should have the foot nearest to the ball up on the line of scrimmage. Then it will be out of the way.

I have little hesitation in saying that the men who are late in lining up after each play are more often guards than anybody else. Why it should be so I cannot say, unless it is that guards, often chosen for the position because they have weight, are slow-moving because of that weight.

No coach, however, who knows his business will place men at guards merely because they have poundage, if he has any other kind of men at hand that will at all do. At any rate it is worth while giving the guards an extra caution to be sure they get lined up as quickly as anybody else and not be crossing to their position behind the snapper at the exact instant that the ball is going into play.

Nowadays many coaches have either one or

both of the guards come out in the interference. This means they drop backward out of their places on the scrimmage line the instant the ball is snapped and, if possible, pace the back-field in getting out toward the end. There they attempt to cut down the loose center or the fullback of the defensive team. To do this a guard would have to be a fast man, and the difficulty of finding men who can do this is great. But when a guard is found who is both powerful and fast he is a mighty asset to his team.

To get out of the line in time to head the end interference not only calls for a large man who is a sprinter, but it also means that he must have considerable grace and nimbleness. Otherwise the footwork required in getting out of the line in the shortest possible space of time will be beyond him. Like the sprinter on the mark, he must learn how to get started in the proper direction with the smallest possible loss of time, and hence much coaching is given the guard in the matter of footwork on offense.

The fault to guard against in trying to get out of the line quickly is the taking of false and unnecessary steps. No matter how short they may be they still take up time, and every second counts. It is as easy to cross the far foot over the nearest one in one great swing, thereby getting in one full stride on your initial movement, as it is to take half a dozen mincing little steps in an endeavor to turn around. This big cross-step will turn a man around instantly in the direction he wishes to go and he will be covering ground at the same time.

If the play is going to the right, and the right guard comes out in the interference, of course, he leaves a gap at the spot he vacated. This gap the left guard, on a balanced line formation, should never forget to fill up as he in turn crosses to the right. All he needs to do is to thrust his elbow into that open place as he goes. That will be sufficient to check the charger, for the latter will not have counted on anything barring his way so soon after he discovered the opening through which he mistakenly figured he could lunge without opposition.

Guards have nothing to do with stopping forward passes by the opponents save to charge through and hurry the passer. But on offense, when an unbalanced line is used, the guard (who is the real middle man of the unbalanced line) is often designated to go out and back up forward passes, holding himself in readiness to head off and tackle any opponent who may attempt to intercept that pass. On balanced line, the center is more often the player who is instructed to perform the work of protecting the pass.

On the defense a guard generally plays very low, almost on one knee. He charges low and hard and quick and *straight ahead*—no matter what the opposing formation. And the guard carries his charge through. The instant he feels hard resistance he should surmise that the attack is going to be directed squarely at him or in his near vicinity. When he feels this resistance he should, after crowding home his charge as far as possible, fall flat, or rather, set lower still, with his head thrust forward, grabbing legs, staying under there, digging his cleats in behind him for dear life, and scramble the opponents in such a way that their runners cannot get through but must dive over the top in the effort to gain.

When the guard feels sure that an end run is coming off, he may set somewhat higher and even attempt at times to knife through—though always on the outside of his opponent. That's a dangerous play to attempt. But, if successful, the guard has accomplished much for his team.

## Tackle.

The tackle position is supposed to be the most difficult on the football rush line.

The physical and moral qualities required of the man who aspires to play the position successfully are unusual and difficult to find. In the first place an ideal tackle is a man standing not less than six feet tall and no less than 190 pounds in stripped weight. Of course there have been mighty fine tackles of shorter stature and of less weight than I have named, but I have mentioned the ideal measurements. Tackles must be very powerful—of rugged, bony frame, and able to stand like iron bridges and hold their feet and position against any force hurled against them. This means that they must have unlimited stubbornness in their make-up.

The tackle is the keystone of each wing. If he caves in the whole side crumples. The college and coaches look to the tackle to play the fiercest brand of ball of most any man on the team. They expect him to lead the way to victory with the aggressiveness of an irritable rhinoceros and the tenacity of a bulldog. He must be a fine diagnostician of plays, an unstoppable charger and a fiendish tackler.

While huge reliance is placed on what a tackle can do in offensive play his main usefulness shows on defense. To play the position with anything like fair results, a man almost invariably needs to have had at least a year or two of high-grade experience as a guard or center before undertaking the great responsibilities of tackle work. After he has learned how to stop them at guard he can be tried out at tackle if he has the requisite shiftiness and spirit.

A tackle should set so wide from his guard as to always tempt the opposition to think it can aim a blow between him and his guard. When that is tried they must be shown by the tackle to have made a faulty guess, for the reason that, no matter how great was the gap between the tackle and guard, the tackle was able to close it after the opposition had been lured toward it. Just how much of a gap a tackle can so safely leave as a trap depends partially on his own height and reach, somewhat on the character and power of the plays, a whole lot on his own shiftiness but—more than anything else—on his ability to charge in with terrible power and aggressiveness and close the door again.

If a tackle can successfully play a very wide game, it's almost impossible to pull off end runs against his team, because the offense has then to get around and outside of the tackle as well as the end—circumventing two men instead of only one. And so the ideal tackle is the man who can play very wide yet not be blocked out when a heavy buck is aimed inside of him.

Formerly, tackles were coached to stand a bit high. They studied the formation of the backs, then fended them off with the arms stiff and rigid until they could ascertain which way the play was going to develop. If it was a run around his own side he knifed across and helped the end to head it off and turn it in. If it was a buck through center he rammed the opposing tackle or guard into the enemy's center and tried to telescope the line so as to tighten it beyond penetration. If it was a buck aimed squarely at him, he instantly dove straight at and under the center of gravity of the attack. If an end run going away from him he cut back behind his own line and helped to back up the other side of the line.

The old system meant that the tackle had to make up his mind just how the play was going to unfold before he could choose which course of action he would take.

Well, that method of playing tackle is still taught in some schools. But the more modern idea of the best way to play tackle on defense is almost diametrically opposed to the old style. The present day trend of tackle coaching is to exhort him to pile in like "a ton of brick" at the very first glimmer he gets that the ball has gone into play. If he can tell what is coming so much the better. But if he cannot tell it makes no difference. He still rushes in with all the speed, power and ferocity he can assemble in his charge and cuts up "like a bull in a china shop."

This means he never cuts behind his own line to make a tackle on the other side of center. But this lack is much more than compensated for by the fact that he has driven his wing of the enemy's line back and away from the scrimmage line so that the opposing backs are meeting a retreating rush line instead of romping on behind one that is advancing—and that makes all the difference in the world when it comes to saying whether a backfield is going to gain ground or not.

It is the writer's profound conviction that a tackle should charge instantly when the ball is passed, with no hesitation whatsoever, and with all the power and sustained effort he can bring to bear.

On offense a tackle must do his full share to open up holes in the opposing line for his backs. Sometimes he teams up with the adjacent guard to take the opposition guard back. Again he takes the opposition tackle and turns him out; it depends on the nature of the play that is to come off. Occasionally, he is not needed at all against a particular rush line opponent and then he must, of course, go through and take a man in the secondary defense.

Tackles should remember at all times that while it looks good from the stands to see them go through and cut down a secondary defense man, their primary duty is to see to it that they have first entirely disposed of the opponents on the primary line of defense. Otherwise the opposing linemen will go through and get your runner behind the line as you were getting their secondary man.

Tackles hurry all attempts to forward pass, except when they are sure the pass is going to be a short one right over their heads. In that case they may often back up and try to get the pass themselves. But they should always make sure at such times that the opposing man with the ball, instead of forward passing, doesn't tuck it under his arm and scoot for five or ten yards right through the vacant tackle hole.

Tackles are also counted upon heavily to

make valiant efforts to block punts, for which purpose they must get out much wider than when opponents line up for their close formation attack. When his own side punts the right tackle usually stays and blocks, but the left tackle is often sent down field in a hurry to help nail the punt catcher in his tracks.

It's a difficult and grand position to play, and there have been plenty of wonderful tackles through the ages—Cowan, of Princeton, Bloomer and Hogan, of Yale, Wauseka, of the Indians, Cutts, of Harvard, Schulte, of Michigan, and a host of others.

## End.

In no department of football play has more progress been made than in the technic of playing end. It is a position calling for peculiar qualifications and splendid judgment, coupled with good speed, nerve and lots of hand skill.

Formerly the physical build of an end made little difference, provided he had speed, grit and good tackling ability. I recall the excellent Yale team of 1891 with the giant Hartwell on one end and the almost diminutive Hinkey on the other. Both were wonderful ends—to my mind the best of the year.

But nowadays we want tall men at the extremities if we can possibly get them. We want them able to reach up into the clouds and pull down forward passes, and hold onto them after they get them down. If they have strong and rugged frames in addition so much the better; but certainly speed and ability to cover territory is as valuable a desideratum as ever.

Twenty-five years ago ends, on defense, played "miles" from their nearest neighbor, the tackle; but all that is changed now. Pennsylvania was the first team to experiment with fetching the ends in close on defense, and they made such a success of the thing that it was not long till nearly all teams began to copy this style of end play, shooting this unhampered man as rapidly as possible across the line of scrimmage and into the opposing backs.

Fears were, naturally, felt at first that the opposing halves would get around these headlong close-in ends for long gains before a secondary defense man could get out to the end to head them off. To guard against that possibility guards were coached to get out and tackle at the ends. And even today the loose center is expected to get out there and help stop circling at the ends.

But the whole proposition of defense against end runs was made to look safe by reason of the fact that, when the forward pass came into the game, the halves had to be moved out to a position behind the ends in order to be where most of the forward passes would come. Being out there, these halves were in splendid position to support their ends in the matter of nailing end runners after the defensive end had forced them into the open by smashing the interference.

It's the business now of an end rush to smash interference on end runs coming his way, **if he can get two or more men by going under it.** If, however, it comes to him loose and scattered so that he could probably get only one man by going under it, his best plan is to keep his feet, stave it off with his hands and arms and fight it back till he has chased the runner out of bounds.

The runner may often elect to try to cut inside rather than continue on till he has gone out of bounds. Here is where the end should forcibly throw aside the interferer whom he has been fending off and take an inward dive at the runner. Often he can get this runner if he judges his time and distance correctly, is fearless and prompt and will leave his feet.

An end never cuts around behind his own line on defense, but *always* takes two steps across the line of scrimmage into opponents' territory, then cuts in sharply and goes fast and hard. If the play is going away from him he chases after it—keeping his eyes wide open in fear of a double pass that may whip back right at him, and which the end must be prepared to tackle for a loss. But all the while he must run hard and try to catch and nail the runner from behind if that runner keeps on around the opposite end.

The end must get out wider whenever the

other team takes kick formation, otherwise it will be easy for the opposition to circle him with a sweeping end run, in case its kick formation merely masks an intended end run.

If the end is sure it is going to be a bona fide punt, and the ball is deep in enemy territory, the thing to do is to go up on the line and try to help block the kick. If they take punt formation while the ball is within his 25 or 30 yard line it is probably NOT a punt, for if it were it would be very likely to roll across his goal line for a touchback; and so again he goes up on the line, but this time because he suspects a long end run, and he must be up there to tackle.

But in midfield or neutral territory his actions will be governed by the situation. If it is fourth down and they have as much as four or five yards or more to go they are almost certain to punt, and in that case it wouldn't be a bad idea for him to drop back about five yards and block the opposing end as the latter comes down under the punt.

Another difficult trick an end must learn is how to box the tackle. This is a maneuver quite often resorted to when a team on the offense wishes to pull off an end run. Here the great danger is the opposing tackle, who must be safely held in check first of all. This is done by having the end help his own tackle to turn and hold that other tackle in. To do this he should, of course, set outside the defensive tackle, and when the latter charges the offensive tackle the end should dive into him low and pin him in. It must be done hard. He must not hit the tackle merely a glance blow, for such will not hold him. *Hard*—that's the thing!

And still another important duty of the end is to get down the field under punts. He gets out a bit wider than usual to do this and he starts at top speed the instant the ball is snapped. He goes down on a line parallel to the side line and aims to **keep always on the outside of the catcher,** thereby turning the catcher inward so he must run the middle of the field. At the middle the end always can get help, for the five center men are coming down the middle. But let a runner once get outside the end, the latter gets no help whatever from his teammates and the ball is often carried back the whole distance it was kicked, or goes altogether for a touchdown. So an end in getting down field must never run straight at the catcher but always on a convex curve, and he should tackle the catcher from the side. The other end is, of course, doing the same thing on his side.

Do your fast running at the start, then you will be down there by the time the ball arrives and you will have a chance to slow up a bit right at the finish. This will enable you to respond to the dodging of the runner better than if you are under full headway, which you will necessarily have to be if you loaf at the outset. As you go down you can permit yourself one very brief glance over your shoulder, mid-way down, in order to get an idea of the general direction and whereabouts of the ball. After that you must learn where it is and where to run solely by an intent study of the men trying to handle the punt.

In going for forward passes try to get away from opponents, as in basketball; but when the other team is making forward passes there is more responsibility resting on you to hurry the passer than on any men in any other positions on your team.

The greatest ends, perhaps, have been Hinkey, Hartwell and Shevlin, of Yale, Hallowell, of Harvard, Exendine, of the Indians, Scarlett, of Pennsylvania, Higgins, of Penn State, Snow and Garrels, of Michigan, and White, of Princeton.

### Quarterback.

Quarterback?

I had almost said there's no such animal. He's an almost extinct species in football. This prehistoric biped once squatted behind, and, if possible, beneath the snapperback. He took every snap made and then passed it to some third individual—usually a back. This "third man'' receiver system was necessary under the old rules. But now that the second man may run with the ball nearly all teams are relying entirely on direct snaps from the center for any and every kind of play, and so the quarterback, in point of fact, is rapidly being eliminated.

The quarterback was invariably the man who called the signals on offense. But today any man with the right amount of gray matter in his skull may call signals, especially if he plays somewhere in the backfield. The man that plays so-called full back is nearly always in an even better position to do this work than the once close-up quarter, because he has a better bird's eye view of the opposing team, which should help any field general considerably.

On my own teams, I haven't used an old-time quarter for over ten years. With me, as with many another coach nowadays, the fourth man in the backfield who would formerly have been called a quarterback is now a second fullback. He shares with the latter the work of plunging, although there is no reason why a fullback could not do some end running if he has the speed or why a half should not do some plunging if he can get up the proper momentum. With me they are absolutely interchangeable men; so I will discuss here the work of the fullback rather than of the quarter.

The mechanical work of this quarter-fullback consists, in the main, of line plunging. His work is complementary to that of the halfback, whose big job is to get around the ends. As before noted, a so-called quarter might easily be a third end runner. But it is much better to have two buckers in the backfield than three end runners. End runs may not be attempted as often as bucks, for it's too exhausting. Though successful end runs usually result in much longer gains than do the bucks, the latter are absolutely essential as a foil to the end running. Otherwise no team would ever be able to run ends, for opponents would stretch their line out—if they found they had nothing to encounter but end runs—till one couldn't get around the extremity even with the speed of antelopes.

A bucker should put his head down and hit with the top of it. He should not run high into the line and try to knife through. He must ram through. But putting his head down doesn't mean that he is to shut his eyes. On the contrary, he keeps them wide open. Even though his head is low as he advances to the line, he is peering out through his eyebrows, and only at the very instant of hitting obstructions does he give his head the final dip that results in the top of his skull becoming the arrow-head that pierces the mass.

A bucker should be a quick starter, and he must be a man able to get up full steam almost instantly. He has but a few yards in which to acquire this 100 per cent momentum. So he must have boundless energy. Momentum is what he needs to make an impression.

For the mass end of the proposition we select preferably a man weighing from 170 pounds up, and for the speed we do the best we can. Then this man must have intelligence, a good memory, nimble brains, eyes to see—and he must be quick to take advantage of opportunities presented. He must have excellent coordination of brain and brawn. He must be a bull for strength, and he must know how to turn that strength loose.

When that man hits the line it should shiver from one end to the other. To be sure, the other backs are usually sent ahead to blaze the way, but ofttimes they fail to open a clean hole for him and when they do not the impact of his onslaught should be the final word needed on the subject. The mass should part under his withering shock as though he had uttered the magic words, "Open Sesame."

On going through, a bucker should have the ball not only tightly under one arm but, at the instant the crash comes, he may well help to hold it firmly with the aid of the other hand. Instantly after he begins to feel lessened pressure against him and more room, he should take the second hand off the ball and begin to thrash about like a buzz saw with that free hand and elbow in order to carve out room and passage for himself. Also he is working his legs like steam pistons, raising his knees high and caring little who nor what they hit so he maintains a firm footing.

He must keep his feet well spread and under him all the time, and take thought as to the maintenance of his balance. Once through, he should raise his head again ever so slightly in order that he may peer out from under his eyebrows and note what the "lay of the land" is before him. If another opponent looms up right in front it is best to lower his head and ram instantly, with all possible force, right into the would-be tackler's stomach. If, however, there seems to be some chance for a dodge or side step, he must plot his field like a flash, decide where his best directions lie, straighten a bit and make off like a halfback.

The fullback is always counted upon heavily to do herculean work in blocking off tacklers for the halfbacks on runs around end. For this work also he should be heavy, quick, willing and eager. He turns the end in or out according to whether it is going to be a long or short end run. He does that by leaving his feet and hitting the end at or about the knees, endeavoring to cut the legs out from under his opponent as a skillfully wielded scythe would fetch down ripe grain.

Naturally, the fullback frequently figures conspicuously when it comes to forward passes. If he is a good passer he may be called upon to make some of them, whereas, if the opponents are trying them he will have to do a man's share to help break them up.

I will not here go into the subject of forward passing, reserving that for separate treatment; but it may as well be said in passing that quarters and fulls should all learn how to forward pass, for so they make themselves much more valuable to their teams.

On defense every backfield man is supposed to be able, not merely catch forward passes, but to size them up before they ever come off. He must be quick and heady in covering the man or men to whom they appear to be going, able to either reach high or jump high and break them up and, in general, to have in that department of the game about as much basketball ability as football talent. It's a very good thing indeed for one who is ambitious to become a star football end or back to play basketball in the winter.

Whether it be the so-called quarter or the full that is giving the signals, the subject of signalling is far too deep and intricate to be discussed here, and it will, therefore, be preserved for later presentation. The same goes for punting, which is not necessarily the fullback's job any more than the quarter's—or any other player. Felton, of Harvard, and DeWitt, of Princeton, both linemen, did about all the punting for their respective teams.

The greatest quarters of the past have, perhaps, been Eckersall, of Chicago, Barrett, of Cornell, Stevenson, of Penn, and Daly, of Harvard, while marvelous fullbacks were Coy, of Yale, Brickley and Mahan, of Harvard, Brooke and Hollenback, of Pennsylvania.

### Halfback.

Halfbacks are usually the fastest men on a football team.

A halfback, in the main, is relied upon to dart around the ends. And to circle end safely in these days of scientifically developed defensive end play, calls for blinding speed whether any other requisites are named or not.

The build of a halfback is immaterial provided he is heavy enough to stand the usual wear and tear of the game. There have been some very fine halfbacks who were heavy enough to do high-grade line bucking and at the same time fast enough to circle the ends. Note the contrast between the two star halfbacks of Georgia Tech of 1917, Strupper, weighing 149, and Guyon 195, both most wonderful players.

A halfback to be successful must also be a good dodger or side stepper. He should be skillful in giving tacklers the stiff arm and, if possible, he should have some trick of spinning out of a tackler's clutch, or of changing his speed so as to make the tackler miscalculate his dive.

Another point of importance in the makeup of a good halfback is to know how to follow and make use of interference. It is often said of halves that they are flashy and showy and want to do it all alone; that they will not make use of their interference but break from it to plunge through some small opening short of the objective that the play calls for. This is a bad fault. The interference was formed especially for the halfback's benefit, and though he may indeed be brilliant enough to make ground without the help of interference he should have sense enough to see that if he can make ten yards without help he could easily make twenty with assistance. On the other hand, it would be a pity to hold a fast half to a pace slower than his best merely because his interference was too slow for him. In such case a change of some sort should be made in the formation which will give the interference a greater lead on this extra fast back.

A halfback must pick floated snaps out of the air with sureness and dependability; he must be free of the venial fault of fumbling. He should be able to lower his head when he gets in a crowd and ram through it much as does a fullback. And he must not slack up to dodge, for there is a whole field full of men thundering in his rear all the time. He should remember, when he gets so close to the boundary that he cannot gain further, that he should go out of bounds with one foot or hand upon the side line as he goes down. This will let his center take the ball out 15 yards at once and give his team operating room for the next succeeding few plays.

A halfback should be a tireless runner. Football is not so much a Marathon run as it is fifty dashes of fifty yards each. He must be a quick starter. He should realize that to circle an end safely it is necessary to clap on spurs the instant the ball is snapped and race away like mad. He cannot hang back, feeling for his opening, else some one will nail him from behind. **If he is going to the right he should put the ball under the right arm**, so he will have his left hand free to fend off the tacklers, most of whom will now approach him from his left. If he goes to the left he should, for the same reason, put the ball under his left arm.

Interference and dependable blocking of tacklers is a part of the duty of a half as much as of any other man on the team. To be considered a finished player, a halfback will have to learn how to leave his feet, dive into a tackler's knees with his body thrown horizontally across the path of the oncoming tackler, and cut the latter's legs out from under him.

Sometimes we hear it said of one halfback that he will not interfere for his brother half, as the other chap will and does for him. This is very bad business, and is about the worst thing a real football player can have said of him. Indeed, he is not a real player if such a thing can justly be charged against him. He must be as self-sacrificing as any other member of the team, and not think at all of the matter of glory for himself but only of the success of the team.

On defense the halves are usually called upon to play the most delicate and difficult position on the entire team. They generally stand from 5 to 7 yards back of their own end and a little outside of him. Their primary duty is to break up forward passes. Their secondary duty is to come up like a storm when they see it is going to be an end run and tackle the runner. Accordingly, we look to the halves to be good open-field, diving tacklers.

One of the best things a halfback can do in watching out for forward passes is to study the end of the other team. If he seems to be trying to get where he can hit either your tackle or your end, you can with fair safety figure that it is likely to be a buck or a run. Therefore, you may at once dismiss the idea of laying back for a forward pass.

On the other hand, if the opposing end seems to be trying to maneuver into a position where he can get away from your end, he is probably planning to get down field in a hurry in order to get a forward pass. But, in addition, the half, as well as other secondary defense men, should study all the opposing backs. If all of them are less than five yards back, or if, after the ball has been snapped, they all are running less than five yards back of the scrimmage line it can hardly work out into a pass. If, however, one of them seems to be running slightly backward, rather than forward, then watch out for a forward pass. If the opposing end goes away out to one side he is the man to watch. If that other end comes rapidly down field you must turn and go with him and *stay with him* even though he runs twenty yards beyond your goal line.

You may think the passer cannot possibly throw it that far but *he can*. And it's your business to stick with that end, not to try to intercept the pass. That end is the magnet that is going to draw the ball—not you. He knows better than you where the ball is coming, and **he** should be the magnet that should draw you as well as the ball. When it comes, be ready to jump for it and bat it out of reach.

Against punt formation, drop back to 10 or 15 yards behind your scrimmage line. One half usually goes back about 30 yards to help his safety man when a real punt is expected.

Halfbacks, as a rule, get more pounding, slamming and bruising up than any other men on the team, and so they must be men of good grit and nerve. They should learn the eternal go-go-go of the game and learn to follow the ball with the tenacity of blood hounds and the speed of hawks. It's a beautiful position to play.

By almost common consent Jim Thorpe, of Carlisle, is usually regarded as the best all-around half that yet has stepped upon a gridiron.

# CHAPTER V.

## DAILY PRACTICE.

At the beginning of the season the squad should be worked very lightly, and the work should consist of little beyond forward passing, punting, catching punts, going down under punts (but not tackling), grass charging, light tackling, falling on the ball, setting up exercises, etc.

The work along any one line should not be continued to exceptional lengths, else it will prove very irksome in the warm days of early season.

The amount of work given each day can gradually be increased as the men are able to stand more.

Of course, lectures should be held every day or evening off the field, accompanied by blackboard diagramming of plays, but even on the field the coach should let the squad rest every 20 minutes or so, and during the five minute rest period he can be explaining many fine points of the game.

After a few days he can give them a set of

signals and begin teaching them plays. As it takes a long time to get a whole system of plays running smoothly, it is wise to give them a considerable period of signal drilling each day. At first only two or three plays should be explained and worked on. As these are mastered and performed smoothly, about one new play every other day can safely be added so that in two weeks' time the boys are well fortified for scrimmage work, at least so far as a repertoire of plays is concerned.

But do not be in a hurry to start scrimmage work. If possible do not hold any scrimmages till every man expected to participate therein has been out 15 days. The muscles and tendons will not be strong enough to stand anything so strenuous before then, and you will be making haste at terrific cost if you risk your men in scrimmage work sooner than that.

And when you do start about 30 downs are plenty for the first day. If the state of the weather remains pretty even you can add about three more downs each day to the number played the previous day; but if it becomes exceedingly hot you can't add any at all, but may wisely cut down on what you did the day before. On the other hand if it gets cool you could safely add 15 or 20 more downs for that day instead of the three you had planned to add.

When your squad has been toughened up to where it can stand a full course you can follow a program something like this:

Start off everybody with a slow quarter mile around the track. That will get circulation going and will warm and loosen up muscles before anything violent is attempted.

Next take up forward pass practice.

After that the linemen may be sent to the tackling dummies for 15 minutes, while the backs are being drilled in punting, catching, blocking, drop kicking, etc. Then the backs can go to the dummies for 10 minutes while the linemen are sent against the charging frame, or are otherwise drilled on fundamentals of line play, position of feet and hands, diagnosis of play, how to block, how to open up holes, etc.

Next the whole squad should be put through a drill of going down field under punts for about 15 minutes. Then follows a signal drill for all teams of about 20 minutes' duration and, finally, the day's work is completed by a stiff scrimmage.

Just how long the scrimmage should last each day is dependent on a great variety of circumstances and conditions. A team that played a hard game the previous Saturday is usually not fit to scrimmage the following Monday at all. If there is a second Varsity, it can well be lined up against the Scrub, or some other team on that day, while the first Varsity takes things a bit easy. The team's mistakes in the Saturday game are gone over, and they take limbering-up exercises, besides being shown the formations and plays of the team they will meet the coming Saturday. Also this is a good day on which to outline in detail any new plays the coach wishes to use the next Saturday. Plenty of signal drill is good work for that day for the First Team.

The hardest scrimmages of the week are always put in on Tuesday and Wednesday. Thursday often sees a good scrimmage also if the team seems to need it; but, as a rule, coaches begin to let down somewhat on that day, as, apart from the danger of the men getting too much work and going stale, there is always the chance that some valuable players may get injured on that day, in which case the time remaining till the game comes on Saturday will be too short to permit of recovery.

The work on the day before a game should be very light indeed. It may consist of forward pass practice, a little light tackling, punting and handling of punts, goal kicking, grass charging, and a snappy 20-minute signal drill.

It might be pointed out that if nearly all the members of a team have had fairly extended playing experience it is not necessary that they should do as much scrimmage work, week in and week out, as should be given to inexperienced players. For the latter there is no help. One learns football and becomes proficient therein by **playing** it, and no one may ever hope to become a good player without plenty of scrimmaging.

The length of heavy scrimmages on Tuesday and Wednesday depends upon the condition of the men. If they are sore, banged up and crippled, there is no sense in driving them into it even though it be Tuesday, or even though their faults of the previous Saturday do stand in serious need of correction. Also it depends on the time of the season. One certainly would not put a team through a set number of downs per day in September as they would in October.

In general, 120 downs for an afternoon is a good day's work, in fact that is the limit. A full game often takes 150 or more downs; but it is not wise to saddle that much work on a team three times a week—Tuesday, Wednesday and Saturday (the match game itself).

The fundamentals of the game are supposed to have been carefully taught and thoroughly learned in the early training weeks of the season. But a team ofttimes wanders away from first principles. This may come about through the carelessness of either the coach or the players, or because they have altogether abandoned practice thereon. Or it may be because their minds have become focused on team play to such an extent that they have forgotten there is such a thing as individual play which has to be kept in a high state of polish, else theories of team play cannot and will not "pan out."

Accordingly it becomes necessary at such

times to go back to the grinding drill of the early days again—tackling, blocking, falling on the ball and what not. Perhaps it is in the handling of punts they have fallen down; perhaps they fumble worse than they did in the first week, perhaps they have forgotten how to charge. At any rate some time must be taken from team maneuvers, such as signal drill or even scrimmage, and the coaches and players must concentrate for awhile on regaining the lost individual excellence.

But when the eleven once gets to doing all things well, and appears to be in tip-top condition, the hard, day-in and day-out work should not be kept up unceasingly; that leads to overtraining and a breakdown. Now's the time to ease up on them and keep them right where they are. An attempt here to "gild refined gold" will only result in the whole precious team crumbling to sand and running out between your fingers. Much less scrimmage work, much less hard tackling and blocking practice should be had—though it is never safe to let up on signal drill. This should be gone through with every day of the season, for the players can get rusty on their formations and signals with amazing rapidity.

A coach should be careful not to give the men too much football via the ears. They can get overtrained mentally quite as well as physically. It's a comparatively easy thing for a man who knows a lot of football to dole it out to youngsters in such wholesale doses that it is impossible for them to assimilate it that rapidly. They simply can't take it all in that fast, and the first thing one knows they have everything mixed up in their minds, or else they're really tired of the subject and want a let up—just as a boy can eat too much dinner at one time and then feels as though he would never care for any more as long as he lives.

Some coaches, for instance, make use of Sunday to give their squads a long theoretical lecture. Once in a while—with the oxen in the furrough—it does seem as though there were no other way out than to do this. But to make a regular practice of it results in little real good being accomplished. The boys have played a hard game just the day before; they are sore, bruised and pounded up; they are tired physically and mentally, and they just want to rest. They don't like to think of going straight back to that unending grind, and if a coach attempts to force it on them, they won't hear a third of what he says, understand a tenth, or retain a twentieth.

You simply must let the boys have time to recuperate in every way; otherwise you do exactly what the fearful student does when he crams till 2 o'clock every morning for a week, or long past the time when his brain ceases to function properly. He gets little out of the book at those late hours when his brain is worn out, and far better would it be for him if he went to bed at a reasonable hour, slept well, arose early with a refreshed mind and went at it again.

So it is with football.

## CHAPTER VI.

## HOW TO TACKLE, BLOCK, AND FALL ON THE BALL.

Tackling is a subject which must be considered under three aspects: (1) When the runner is coming straight at you; (2) when you have to take him from the side, and (3) when he is going straight away from you.

The first instance is oftenest met with when a bucker is coming through the line. In such a case it is the roving center and the fullback (the two middle men in the secondary line of defense) that have the best opportunity to make the straight-on tackle, although every man on the team also gets many such chances.

As a rule, a tackler should, whenever possible, get dead in front of a runner and tackle him front on. Not only is it easier and surer to tackle a man coming straight toward your arms than when he is going past you to one side, but in the former case when you do get him—if you get him correctly—you throw him back *toward his own goal*. If you have to take him from the side he usually falls his own length toward *your* goal.

89

If it happens that you are well to one side of the runner, at the start, don't defer your tackle until you can outrun him and make a front-on tackle. Get him at the earliest fraction of a second whether it's front-on or side-ways. But remember always that when he is coming down the field you should try to make a head-on tackle.

Here he comes!

You go to meet him, because if you delay he will eat up all the ground between you and him —and that's territory you wish to hold for your own team. Don't look at his feet; watch his hips. Run for him partially crouched and move as rapidly as possible. But always make sure you have such firm control of your legs as to be able to respond suddenly to any sharp dodge the runner may make. Presently you get so close together that you feel another step will bring you into collision and so you cannot miss —he cannot now sidestep you.

Now——

Plant your forward foot straight at him, keeping the rear one well behind, with cleats stuck firmly into the ground, for a brace—so he will not run rough-shod and bodily over you. Bend down sharply, exerting strongly your waist muscles. Reach your arms far around him just above the knees, lower your head so low that it practically touches your forearm, bore in hard with your shoulder and throw the weight and force of your chest—which is the heaviest and strongest part of your body—right into the lacing of his pants.

Instantly you have clamped his knees together with a vice-like grip. In this you are greatly aided by the muscles of the neck, which you bring into the tackle by shoving the side and back of your head hard against the runner's thigh—as a bull would lift with his neck. By clamping the runner's knees together you take from him his broad base.

An upright man is a tall tower, which cannot stand without a wide foundation; take the foundation from under him and he must come down. Now you lift sharply, with a quick, snappy jerk—not a long, slow ponderous pull. Still keeping his legs *together* you pull them out to the same side your head is on; you raise them high in the air, and behold!—his head falls down to the other side, and in this position you can ram his head into the ground as easily as you could thrust a fence post into its newly dug hole.

Novices, in head-on tackling, forget to *lift*. They leave their feet, without any necessity whatever—seeing the man is right dead in front of them—and aim merely to catch hold of his legs and *drag him down,* whereas they should keep their feet, pick the man up and SET him down. If the runner were to one side of them it might be different; but I am not presupposing that case. To do it the way I have outlined above will make it a much surer tackle and an easier one. A tackler must not be lazy about bending all the way down and quickly when the proper time comes, and neither must he be lazy about lifting the runner.

Much academic discussion has been had on whether one should tackle "head-on" a runner coming full front into him, or whether the tackler should turn his head to one side. Now, common sense—and that's what the author tries to use in coaching any phase of football— points out that some players having long, thin necks ought not to be permitted to tackle head-on: they're bound, sooner or later, to get their necks twisted—perhaps badly. On the other hand, it's perfectly true that if you let men tackle with their heads turned off to one side, presently or often they are going to make a one-armed tackle: they won't be boring in close enough to get a good tight hold of their man with *both* arms, and the runner will break through and past that one-arm clutch. One arm alone cannot properly surround a runner's legs.

And so if a man has a good, thick, short, strong neck I urge him to learn head-on tackling; and if he has the other kind I point out frequently to him the necessity for fighting in and getting to close grips with his man, taking care to make no one-handed or "finger" tackles and, in any case, to get his shoulder hard into the runner's middle.

In making a head-on tackle it's easier to pull his feet toward you, bringing them up between your own, instead of out to one side. In every case tacklers should throw *their weight* into the runner: don't be satisfied to pull the man down by hand clutches of his loose clothing. It takes *fighting determination* to become a good tackler: cultivate that determination.

## Side Tackling.

When the man with the ball is scudding by you, sharply to one side and going "great guns," it is freely granted you cannot make a standing, front-on tackle; you have to get him now or never, and get him most any old way you can. The commonest way is simply to dive at his legs just above the knees, diving so hard that you can break down or through his stiff arm, if he tries to give you one, boring in till your shoulder hits his near thigh hard and shoves it over toward his far leg. Simultaneously, you reach out your arms to their utmost extent to catch hold of that far leg and draw it in toward the near one. If the tackler succeeds in doing all these things the runner is bound to come down. His legs have again been clamped and he cannot maintain a footing.

In tackling, the runner is brought to earth not because there is brought to bear against him greater momentum or even greater force, but because the tackler takes away his support. A man doesn't run with his arms or head, but with his legs, and if we can but chain up his legs he will have to stop then and there, no matter if he weighs a thousand pounds and can run a hundred yards in five seconds. In other words, a fine tackle is nothing more nor less than the scientific, highly developed and legal *tripping a man*.

I am sometimes asked whether a side-tackler should thrust his head in front of the runner's legs or behind them. If he is far enough to the front of the runner he should shoot his head in front, although he will have to watch that the runner, in raising his legs, does not strike the tackler with a thigh or knee right on the head. In the "twist" tackle, the tackler coming from right angles to the runner, shoots his body across the path of the runner. He catches that runner's legs with his arms as he shoots by and hangs on for dear life. The propulsive force of his dive results in the runner being spun around in his tracks and being felled to the ground with his head being thrown back toward his own goal, with some danger that the back of his head may hit the ground with considerable force. It's a beautiful and effective tackle to make, but it's difficult as well, and it should not be tried except under the supervision and guiding instruction of an expert adviser and coach. When once thoroughly learned it may be attempted with entire safety in any game.

When chasing a runner from behind you dive after him the same as you would from one side.

Probably you won't catch him at all unless you
do dive, and then you get so much nearer to
him by reason of the length of your body being
added to whatever speed you are getting into
the chase.  Here you stand the risk of getting
a kick in the face with the heel of the runner—
but it's a chance you have to take: It's all in
the day's work.  Don't flinch!

### Tackling by the Safety Man.

The smallest man on a team is usually put
back as defensive safety man.  He should be
fast, a sure handler of punts, and an extra good
man in open field so he may stand a good chance
of bringing back the opposition's  punts for
goodly distances.  Most safety men play back
too far most of the time.  Twenty-five to thir-
ty yards back is enough, as a rule. This will render it posible for you to intercept many forward
passes that would fall short of your position
if you were back farther.

But  about tackling for you: Of course you
understand you should be a dead-sure tackler,
for you are the last hope of your team.  Yes,
you are little and he is big; so you must have
nerve—lots of it.  Remember that he is bother-
ed with the ball, and that you, having had more
moments of rest during  the progress  of the
game than he, are not so tired as he.  In the
first place, you have run up to meet him close
to your scrimmage line, and so perhaps you will

have some help from your teammates if you can but make him hesitate, make him lose distance to dodge, or even merely make him stumble: take courage from these flashing reflections and—go for him like a game cock.

NOW—as he comes, deliberately step toward the middle of the field from him, thus *forcing* him to go between you and the nearest boundary. Then he will not have a choice of *three* ways of going at you—right, left or straight on; no, he will have only one way, and that will be to go between you and that boundary line, either by force or by sheer speed. But you count on that boundary line: he is your sure friend—the deadliest tackler on the field. As the runner nears you, you close in on him, steadily forcing him nearer the boundary in order to avoid you and, finally, you crowd him clear out of bounds, or else you nail him absolutely because in avoiding the boundary he had to come into you.

## How to Interfere.

Every school boy that ever saw football knows that by "interference" we mean the aid which a player gives, or tries to give, to his teammate carrying the ball by clearing a way for him through or around opponents. An "interferer," being offside, may not use his hands or arms to keep away the tacklers of the other side but he may use his body for this purpose.

Formerly interferers could think of no other or better way to so use the body than to run on ahead of, or alongside, their runner and bump into opponents with the shoulder. In other words, they endeavored to "shoulder" the tacklers out of the way. To this good day this form of "blocking" (as interference is more commonly called) is favored by some coaches, on the theory that a blocker is, by this method able to remain on his feet and so keep on and get a second and even a third man and "shoulder" them out of the play also. As a theory it does indeed listen good; but as a practical working fact it is, in the opinion of the writer, a dismal failure.

It presupposes that a man who may not use his hands or arms at all is the superior of a defensive man who may use both to their fullest extent. And as the interferer who relies solely on bumping the tackler out of the way seldom or never succeeds in doing so—against first-class opponents—whether he ever gets a second or third tackler is of no consequence when he failed to get the first one, for that first tackler nails his runner behind him and the play is all over.

In studying for a surer method of blocking tacklers, coaches began to learn that it lay in taking away the legs of the prospective tackler. It's a bit harder trick to cut the legs out from under a man when you may not have the help of your hands or arms in executing the trick.

But it can be done—and is being done. Dropping in front of an onrushing tackler usually trips him—and down he goes, no longer a menace to your own runner.

Correct blocking and correct tackling are exactly the same thing, except that in the latter case you may use your hands and arms to help out, while in the former department of play you are stopped altogether by rule from laying hands upon a tackler whom you are endeavoring to head off.

In blocking a tackler you dive *in front* of him, shooting your body cross-wise or at right angles to his upright body. You leave your feet, keeping every joint rigid and stretching yourself out to your full length—so that your whole body is straight from the top of your head to the sole of your feet. Keep it so, parallel to the ground. You do this so as to get the full benefit of your entire height—or length, rather—in trying to block up his path, whereas if you curl up like a ball he easily steps around one or the other end of you.

Keep your whole body stiff and rigid so that it moves with the impact of your entire weight, whatever that may be. If you let your joints hang limp and loose you only hit him with so much of your mass as is contained between the joints on either side of the spot where your anatomy collided with his, whereas, if you allow no joints or hinges to be in your body at that instant, then you hit him with your whole weight.

Your hip is the part of your anatomy you should throw into his legs, if possible.

It's very necessary that you learn just when and where to take off in making your dive at a man. To do this you will not only have to know about how far you are from him and your own speed, but also about what you think his speed is. so that you will be able to figure your meeting point. If you miscalculate this you are very liable to miss him altogether no matter how clever your dive. You must get close enough to him so that after you dive he does not have time to side-step you before your body strikes his legs. On the other hand if you wait too long you are still on your feet and that will mean that you are not low enough to get him where his legs can be cut out and you will not have force enough.

In bringing a scythe around against standing grain you must have noticed that the reaper swings the blade low and with a swift swing that cuts the whole stalk off neatly close to the ground. Were he to attempt to cut off only the tops of the stalks his blade would not meet with the same rooted resistance as it encounters close to the ground, and he would often fail to behead the stalks.

This illustrates why you should go low.

"Clipping" is shooting your body horizontal-

ly across the legs of an opponent *from behind.*
It is now prohibited: don't do it.

It is highly essential that every man on an
eleven should become a clever and dependable
blocker. With such defense as is seen on every
field nowadays it is practically impossible for
a player, no matter how brilliant a runner and
dodger he may be, to gain any ground whatever
without yeoman blocking assistance from his
teammates.

And the most effective way to do such blocking is to take the legs from under them—in the
way I have just described. A good blocker is of
much more worth to his team than is merely a
good runner, for the latter can help his team
only when he happens to take the ball while the
good blocker can help *every* time the ball
goes into play and no matter which man carries
it.

This point is rapidly beginning to be understood by the general public and due credit is
being given the clever blocker. Formerly spectators who understood nothing of the fine
points of the game, saw nobody but the man
running with the ball and gave him the credit
for his long run, whereas it came about usually as the result of fine interference from his fellows.

So far as the tackler is concerned, he must be
ever on the alert for diving blockers, and he
should endeavor to mislead them as to **just**

where he will be at a given instant of time so
that they will miscalculate their dive. If he can
do this he will probably be able to get around
one end or the other of the diver without great
loss of time. Should he not succeed in this,
however, the only thing he can do is to stiff-arm
the body of the blocker off from his knees and
force it down to the ground, after which he can
quickly leap over the prostrate body. If he allows his opponent's dive to carry clear in
against his knees he is almost certain to be cut
down.

## How to Carry the Ball.

This is a point usually overlooked by the
average player, but one of vast importance
nevertheless. Possession of the ball is not only
nine but ninety-nine points of the game, for if
one could hold to, and retain possession of the
ball the entire game they could not possibly
lose the game otherwise than by making a safety. Accordingly it behooves a team never to
lose possession as the result of mere carelessness when a little attention to the detail of what
is the right and what the wrong way to hold and
carry a ball will result in infrequent loss thereof through fumbling.

Many allowances may at times be made for a
player failing to get a snapped or passed or
punted ball, but when he once secures and has it
no excuse can be tolerated for fumbling or giv-

ing it up again as the result of a sloppy style of holding the spheroid. And so, assuming there was nothing the matter with the snap and that the runner caught it alright, the next thing to consider is what he should do with it. He should instantly, but carefully, transfer it to the outside arm and thrust one end of the ball very snugly up into the armpit on that side. The other end of the ball should be enclosed in the hand on that side while he closes down hard on the ball with both his forearm and upper arm, at the same time pulling the ball forcibly up into his armpit still more tightly. This firm grip he should maintain on the ball until he is down, always subconsciously keeping in his mind the value of the precious burden he is bearing. This, of course, is carrying the ball with one arm and hand in end running. The style one sees occasionally of the runner carrying the ball before him in both hands is very dangerous; an unexpected bump or jar or tackle is liable to forcibly pull one hand or other away from the ball and then it must fall to earth immediately.

For bucking purposes it is well to carry the ball more over the pit of the stomach, with both hands holding the ball until the bucker is fairly through the line, when he may straighten up and get it up under one armpit for open field running and dodging, if he thinks he has a chance. However, if he will get the ball up under the armpit as snugly as I would wish him to do and then hold to the ball hard he will do well to carry it that way even when bucking, and so have one arm free to help him forge a way through the line, or with which to rid himself of secondary defense tacklers the instant he gets through.

## About Falling on the Ball.

Some authorities prefer to coach players nowadays to pick up fumbles neatly and gallop off with them rather than to fall on the loose lying ball and make sure of possession. The former is the proper thing to do if one is off to one side with the ball and opponents are not near enough to hurry you in your hasty snatching at the crazy thing; and also this may more safely be attempted by old and experienced players than by green and unseasoned men. But if the ball is in the midst of a mad scramble of opposing players one stands very little chance of getting it at all by any other method than by instantly diving for it and covering it with the body.

In attempting this one should dive as low to the ground as posssible. This will get you to the ball more quickly and will not result in your getting so hard a drop to the ground as would be the case were you to leap upward first and then drop three or four feet. But the consideration of even greater importance is that by going in low you are often able to shoot in beneath a man who is actually nearer the ball than yourself but who has gone at it with a high dive. By shooting low you simply slide in under him and get there quicker.

The idea in diving on the ball thus is not instantly to get your hands on it but to thrust your hands beyond it and pull it in toward you at the same time that, by your dive, your body is sliding and so advancing toward it. You do not dive flat on your stomach, but turn on your side as you shoot and then draw the ball in toward your short ribs as you simultaneously curl your arms, body and thighs around it. In a word, you draw up your legs, bend you head, neck and shoulders down and curl up around the ball just like a porcupine. Then hang on for dear life, for opponents will no doubt reach under you and still try to "steal" the ball from you. Just lie there clutching that ball as though it were a gold nugget of similar size until the referee awards it to you.

If you feel no one falling on you of course you lose no time then in springing to your feet and making off.

## Catching Punts.

So many players try to handle a punted football as they would a fly baseball—with the hands; and that is all wrong. A football is not round like a baseball and it will not come down or travel through the air evenly as does the lat-

ter.  You can't tell how it is going to wobble
and, anyway, it is too large an object  for the
fingers and hands alone securely to grasp.

The best way to catch a punt is to  make a
small basket of the hands and forearms, or at
least these make the sides of the basket, while
the pit of the stomach makes the bottom of the
basket.  In other words you let the ball come
clear into the abdomen and strike there, and
simultaneously with its striking the body you
clap your hands on the outside of the ball and
keep it there.  An equally good way is to hold
one hand under the other so that the ball cannot
slip through altogether, and let it land partly
against the abdomen and partly on the lower
hand.  If you will try this method you will find
that you can get the ball up under the arm of
the underneath hand much more quickly than
if the hands are held on an even keel.

## Stiff-Arming an Opponent.

Few players have the natural  instinct  to
make use of the free arm, when running with
the ball, in order to fend off a tackler; and so
this art has generally to be taught young players and they have to be "bawled out" about the
failure a good deal before they get to remembering.

The idea is, when you note a tackler coming
up into you fast and hard, to thrust out your
free arm at its fullest length to ward him off.

If you wait to extend your arm until he gets real close to you you will find yourself unable to open out your arm and keep him at arms' length, for you will then have to shove him off with your bent arm before you can get it stretched out to its full length, and he will be coming with such force that you will be quite unable to do this. It's like operating the blade of a jackknife. If you have the blade only partially opened any little force on the back of the point will suffice to close it up; but if you have the blade opened clear out you can thrust powerfully with the point just as though there were no hinge or joint there at all.

And where do you thrust your hand at the end of your stiff arm? Squarely into the tackler's face, if he presents it to you as a target. His business is to lower his head and not keep his face exposed, for he should tackle low anyway. No, you do not jab your clenched fist into his face, but you have a perfect right to thrust your spread fingers full at his face and he must take the consequences. If he lowers his head you will have to place your hand against the top of his head, and at the instant that you shove hard, *still keeping your arm very stiff and rigid*, you draw your hips and legs away from his tackle so he will not be able to get you with his arms. In other words you should use this stiff arm jab not only to push him back but also to push yourself away from him, just as a boatman would use a pole to push his boat away from a pier.

Try to push the tackler's head down into the ground. A man's body will follow where his head leads—just as a tricycle follows the direction taken by the little wheel in front. And see if you can't, while thrusting your hand at the tackler, put your shoulder behind the thrust and your whole upper body as well—much as a shot-putter does.

# CHAPTER VII.

## HEISMAN'S FOOTBALL AXIOMS.

### On Offense—Dont's.

1. Don't try to play without your head.
2. Don't habitually holler "Signal"—*Listen*.
3. Don't forget the signals.
4. Don't be late in lining up.
5. Don't have your feet in the way of the snapback.
6. Don't play loose or wide line.
7. Don't let your opponent get the charge on you.
8. Don't look toward where the play is going.
9. Don't lean or incline; set squarely.
10. Don't jab your fingers into a snapped ball.
11. Don't catch it on your wrists.
12. Don't let it hit you on the chest.
13. Don't coil your arm around its belly.
14. Don't hold it on your stomach: you can't run so.
15. Don't stick it out in front when you are downed.
16. Don't forget to hold it tightly in a crowd.

17. **Don't fumble** it; you might better have died when you were a little boy.
18. Don't hesitate about falling on it ever.
19. Don't forget to pull it loose from an opponent.
20. Don't ever give ground to get by a tackler.
21. Don't slack up to dodge.
22. Don't forget to stiff arm.
23. Don't hesitate which hole to take.
24. Don't go into the line with your head up.
25. Don't use your arms or shoulders to block.
26. Don't fail to get out of bounds when near it.
27. Don't see how light you can hit, but how hard.
28. Don't cuss, and don't be unsportsmanly ever.
29. Don't argue with the officials; it's the captain's job.
30. Don't lose the game.

## Defensive Don'ts.

1. Don't play close or tight line.
2. Don't forget to study the backs.
3. Don't overlook an opponent laying out.
4. Don't ever turn your back on the play.
5. Don't charge inside your opponent.
6. Don't be afraid of over-shifting.
7. Don't let your opponent get the jump on you.
8. Don't charge with less than your full force.

9. Don't charge high except when you **are**
   sure it is an end run, punt or pass.
10. Don't hesitate to go under interference.
11. Don't tackle high.
12. Don't let him slip out or tear loose **after**
    you have him.
13. Don't fail to put the runner down always.
14. Don't stop running because you're behind.
15. Don't fail to follow the ball **all** the time.
16. Don't let a double pass fool you.
17. Don't stop going into a passer or kicker **as**
    long as he still has the ball.
18. Don't fail to block the ends on a kick by
    opponents.
19. Don't let a runner get outside of you.
20. Don't try to stop interference with **your**
    fingers or hands.
21. Don't let your line opponent get a leg hold
    on you.
22. Don't forget to use your hands in break-
    ing through the line.
23. Don't forget to clamp the runner's legs.
24. Don't put him down  easy but hard—al-
    ways.
25. Don't fail to talk encouragingly.
26. Don't hesitate to dive for a runner; it's
    the only way sometimes.
27. Don't let the runner get out of bounds.
28. Don't wait for opponents to come to you.
    Take the battle to them.
29. Don't let one interferer take you off; it's
    ridiculous.

30. Don't "blow;" keep calm, cool and determined—but FIGHT all the way.

"DON'T FLINCH! DON'T FOUL!
AND—HIT THE LINE HARD!"

**Offense** means—Go hard and Block.

**Defense** means—Charge and Fight.

### Use.

1. Use your Brain on both  offense and defense **all** the time.
2. Use your Ears to hear the signals.
3. Use your Eyes to diagnose the play.
4. Use your Mouth to tell your team about it.
5. Use your Head to buck with.
6. Use your Neck to help tackle with.
7. Use your Shoulders to charge with.
8. Use your Hands on defense all the time.
9. Use your Fingers to handle the ball.
10. Use the Straight Arm to ward off a tackler.
11. Use your Elbows to help block on the line.
12. Use your Hips to block a tackler.
13. Use your Stern for nothing but ballast.
14. Use your Legs to run your fastest always.
15. Use your Knee on a diving blocker.
16. Use your Feet to make a broad base and get a firm footing.
17. Use your best Judgment on a new formation.

18. Use your Interferers as dodging posts.
19. Use your Opponent often to smash back the runner.
20. Use his Stomach for a drum: tattoo it with the back of your open hand.
21. Use his Head as a handle to pull or push him by.
22. Use your Muscle to the limit; turn it loose.
23. Use all your Fighting Instinct and get more.
24. Use more than one Way to handle an opponent.
25. Use your Opponent up and yourself as well, till the game is won.

## Always.

1. Always play with your head.
2. Always listen for signal.
3. Always line-up fast.
4. Always charge with the ball.
5. Always run your fastest.
6. Always follow the ball.
7. Always carry ball under armpit.
8. Always cut your man down clean in interfering.
9. Always follow your interference.
10. Always stiff-arm a high tackler.
11. Always cross-step a low tackler.
12. Always tackle low.
13. Always break through on the outside.
14. Always smash interference first, then tackle.

15. Always study opposing backfield.
16. Always vary your method of handling an opponent.
17. Always, on the line, hurry the punter or passer.
18. Always play closer for an expected buck, and lower.
19. Always wider and higher for an expected end run.
20. Always keep track of the down and distance opponents have to gain; it aids diagnosis.

## Can'ts.

1. You can't play superior football without brains.
2. You can't play finished football without knowing the rules.
3. You can't make the team if you don't understand teamwork.
4. You can't play satisfactory ball if you don't know the signals.
5. You can't make a real player without legitimate aggressiveness.
6. You can't do yourself justice without getting and staying in condition.
7. You can't break training rules without sapping your own morale.
8. You can't fight like a man with less than 100 per cent loyalty and college spirit.
9. You can't be a great player if you have the swell head.

10.  You can't afford to loaf any during foot-
     ball season.

## Never.

1.  Never come on the field without your brain.
2.  Never get excited.
3.  Never give up.
4.  Never get tired.
5.  Never play less than your very hardest.
6.  Never expect to make a runner if you slow
    up when opposed.
7.  Never look back when running  with the
    ball.
8.  Never drop the ball.
9.  Never pick up a loose ball in a crowd.
10. Never let an opponent take it away from
    you.
11. Never stop following the ball.
12. Never admit to yourself your opponent is
    a better man than you are.
13. Never interfere with a fair catch.
14. Never throw a man making one.
15. Never let your opponent know what you
    are going to do.
16. Never lose sight of the ball.
17. Never shut your eyes.
18. Never tackle with your head up.
19. Never break Training Rules.
20. Never forget a football player may be a
    gentleman.

### About Punting—The Punter.

1. Never get back less than 10 yards.
2. Never call for the ball till every teammate is in proper position.
3. Don't let yourself be hurried; don't call for the ball till you are calm and ready.
4. Never take your eye off the ball after it's been snapped.
5. Don't jab your fingers at it and poke it away from you.
6. Don't take too long adjusting it in your hands.
7. Never take more than three steps or it will be blocked. Two are enough.
8. Never punt with your toe—always your instep.
9. Don't drop it too close; it will go straight up.
10. Don't let it fall too low—there'll be no force in the kick.
11. Don't hasten if opponents are not rushing you; hold it so as to let your line get down.
12. Always put it out of bounds if in opponents' territory and side line is neither too close nor too far away.
13. Never put it out of bounds if in **your own** territory.
14. Never kick it over opponents' goal line for a touchback.
15. Always back up your own punt.

### About Passing—The Passer.

1. Don't disclose that you are going to pass.
2. Be sure you are 5 yards back when you do.
3. Always back up your own passes.
4. Be sure you know what men are eligible.
5. Beware of making lateral passes; they are dangerous—easily intercepted.
6. Holler "BALL" as you are drawing back your arm.
7. Don't throw it out of bounds.
8. Be sure it clears the rush line—if meant to go beyond.
9. Learn accurately who the preferential catcher is on each pass, and also which man is second choice.
10. Short passes must be gotten rid of quickly.
11. Don't put a maximum of velocity on short ones.
12. Long passes should not be made higher than necessary—they give opponents time to get under them also.
13. All passes should be made so the catcher will have to reach up for them.
14. Don't get excited (by opposing rushers breaking through) into frequent abandonment of the pass, and be frightened into running with the ball instead.
15. Don't throw it wildly or aimlessly to the ground just to get rid of it; you'll be penalized.

## The Catchers.

1. The commonest fault of a catcher is to go down field farther than he has been coached.
2. The next commonest is that he doesn't go in quite the right direction.
3. An ineligible man should try hard to **avoid** being touched by a passed ball.
4. If you can't catch it yourself bluff hard that you are **trying t**o catch it—yet spoil it for opponents.
5. Be prepared instantly to tackle if an opponent gets it.
6. Don't fall on a pass that has grounded.

## When Opponents Try a Pass.

1. Linemen Rush! Rush! Rush the passer your very hardest. **Keep on** going into him till he has rid himself of the ball.
2. Backs make no special effort to catch a pass on last down—unless strongly lateral—but merely spoil it for the opponent. Before last down they do try to catch it.
3. If eligible catcher is about to catch it sprawl on him, but keep looking at the **ball,** not at **him.** This will avoid a foul being called on you.

## Remember:

All games of football are won on the **other** side of the scrimmage line, not on yours.

## CHAPTER VIII.

### SIGNALING SYSTEMS.

All authorities are agreed that the signaling system for a foot ball team should be simple. The only reason why it should not be arises because of the fear that rival teams may be able to penetrate them.   This, it must be admitted, is a possibility—especially if the preliminary games are played on a small field and with the spectators not confined to the stands, because then it is easily possible for an opposition scout to follow the play along the side lines, hear all the signals, take them all down, note what kind of a play followed such and such a complete signal and then decipher the whole series at his leisure after the game is over.

It is also not unlikely that opposition players will figure out the "key" in certain games in which you may be using but a few plays.   These repeated over and over, accompanied each time by a signal that seems to have the same number in it somewhere, come in time to be "spotted."

Some will tell you it is absurd to worry about your signals being deciphered because, they say, no self-respecting scout would listen to a team's

signals, and not one team in a hundred would
try to listen for them and play defensively by
them if they did know its opponents' signals.
Well, I'm sorry; but they're wrong — those
same good folks. Most scouts figure they have
as much right to learn all they can of a team's
play through the use of their ears as by employing their eyes, and that it is perfectly fair
and legitimate for them to  learn  anything
they can of the team's play from the game in the
open and played before the public, although
that same scout might scorn to hide himself
where he could overlook or  overhear  something concerning their  secret  practice,   or
might never even dream of bribing some trait-
or to give him the same information.  Mind
you, I am not defending this position; but I
well know that the signals of teams do get out
and they have been used by opposition teams
in games oftener then is commonly supposed
to have been the case.  So it is well  to  be
careful about the whole thing.

In the early days signals were generally used that consisted merely of casual phrases, as:
"Everybody get into this now," which might
mean that the left half should take the ball
around right end—or around his own end (unassisted) as was not infrequently the case many
years ago.

Then came an improvement in the shape of
a more specialized signal.  In this system the
last letter of the first word told which back
was to get the ball.  If the half backs' letters,

for example, were "k" and "y" respectively, the words "Break through there" and "Knock 'em down" told one thing, while the phrases "Hurry up" and "Try hard everybody" meant different things.

The writer recalls a Marine team he once went up against in the early days, and knowing little or nothing of nautical terms there was no chance in the world for me to ever interpret aright such instructions as, "Port your helm," "Let out your spanker," or Take a reef in the fore-top gallant sail."

Fnally came figures and numbers, and these are in their nature so much more in consonance with the whole spirit of the game that it was not long before every team in the land was employing them, though not till after a few very ingenious systems based on the cardinal distinction between vowels and consonants had been cleverly employed by some teams.

An example of a signaling system that seems to the writer too complicated for most players is one in which a certain number is used to indicate the formation that the team is to take, another number tells which man is to carry the ball, still another directs where he is to go with it, and yet another imparts the information as to just when the ball is going to be snapped. Here are four different numbers that must be taken cognisance of as the quarter rattles them off, and each has a different meaning. On top of that sometimes

a second series of numbers are called in order
to pave the way for the calling of the particular number or digit on which the ball is to
be snapped.

Then we have the other system which goes
to the opposite extreme and which assigns
but one number of those called as having any
meaning at all. This number not only tells
who is to get the ball, but it is understood that
that same number means that the runner is to
go for a certain opening. The same hole assaulted by another runner would call for a
different number, or the same runner going to
a different hole would likewise call for a distinct number. This is easy where the line is
balanced and the backs take the usual balanced, standing formation each time. Or ev-
en if the formation is frequently unbalanced
this can be handled by the signaler simply
calling for "Right Formation" or "Left Formation" before starting on his row of numbers.
In passing, I might as well say here I do not,
in such case, allow my quarters to waste their
valuable breath on repeating over and over
again before each signal the word "formation": it's simpler and means just as much
to say merely, "Right" or "Left."

A more flexible system than the one just described consists in having a certain digit tell
who takes the ball, while another digit directs
where he is to go with it. This system is, probably, in more common use, not only by High
Schools, but by college teams as well, than any

other. For this reason it will be described in some detail. Observe the following diagram:

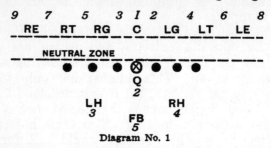

Diagram No. 1

Here you will notice that of one team the backs (Offensive) are set down by initials. Each has been assigned a number. On the other side of the neutral zone we observe that the defensive linemen have been designated by initials, and the spaces or "holes" between them have been given numbers. We note, as we face that defensive line, that the even numbers, 2, 4, 6 and 8 are to our right, while the odd numbers 3, 5, 7, and 9 are to our left.

If we wanted a long run clear around our right end—which really means clear around *their* left end, it is easy to figure out that Hole No. 8 is the one we desire to assail; while if we wish to make a short run of it (or an "off-tackle" play, as it is more often called) we find that the number of the hole so to be assaulted is 6. And so, if we wanted to send our left half around on the first mentioned play, we would have to call out the digit 3 to indicate the left half, and follow it up somewhere with the digit 8 to tell that we want the *long* end run; while if we want him to make an off-tackle smash to the right we would use the digit 6 to indicate the spot to be attacked, coupling it with the left half's number, 3.

In other words, it is to be noted that the numbers of the holes to be assaulted have reference to the seven players of the opposition scrimmage line and not of your own line. Some teams use only eight different numbers for this purpose, not assigning a ninth digit, as I have done, to bear directly over or upon the opposing center; but this is sometimes desirable,—for instance for the purpose of defining more clearly just where a certain forward pass should go.

The perfect elasticity of this system is demonstrated by pointing out that any one of the backs, or all of them, can be shot at a particular spot simply by shifting the backs about so that each shall occupy the favorable or best position or spot on which to receive the snap (or pass from the quarter) and from which to start his drive at the given hole. This is of immense advantage in a game where, say, your quarter has ascertained that one particular man of the opposition is exceptionally weak. With this signaling system in force every man of the back field can be given the ball to hit that particular spot of the defense.

It is apparent that the odd numbers might have gone to the right and the evens to the

left. Again, the digits 1 and 2 might have been
assigned to the end holes, thus bringing the
high number 9 over the center. Also one
might start with the digit 1 at one end
and run the whole nine of them straight
through from right to left, or from left to
right. But the method employed in the diagram is simpler and probably best for general purposes.

If you play an unbalanced line on attack
this will require no change in this method of
signaling. Here comes in the beauty of making the hole numbers have reference to the defense, not to the offense. In the latter case
you might want the two guards on the one
side, or the two tackles, or the two ends, and
in either of these cases it would have been
hard to designate the openings between some
of them without making changes in your system. But the defensive linemen always shift
*as a whole* to meet a shifted attack, and so
the holes between them are always the same,
whether against a balanced or an unbalanced
attack.

Next we inquire how these two all-import-
ant numbers are conveyed in the signal. The
simplest way is to throw them into double
numbers and utilize for that purpose the first
double numbers called as being the significant
one. Thus in 36-75-48 only the first one, 36,
counts for anything, the rest being used merely to disguise the first. In this the first digit
3 would mean that the left half takes the ball,

while the second one, 6, tells that he is to carry it between their left tackle and left end.
After using this first number for the first
week or so of the season a team would likely
change to use of the second, or third, or last
double number called as the significant one.

But the value of a system like this lies
largely, too, in the fact that it is easy to vary
the "key" so that these meaningful digits
may readily be concealed. Thus we might use
the last digit of the first double number called
and the first digit of the second double number called to indicate our purpose, as: 53-69-
47, in which we direct play No. 36. The same
play called for by 39-46-78, shows we are using
as the "Key" the first digit of the first double
number and the last digit of the second double
number. Or it might be the first double number following any number from 10 to 20,
as: 47-98-13-36. Then, again, this system
of numbering players and holes can be handled
by calling out single digits only, as:
3-6-8-5, in which the first and second digits
are the ones for which we are on the lookout.
Or first and third would be, 3-7-6-4; while
second and third would be, 5-3-6-9. An
example of first and last would be: 3-5-2-
8-7-6. Or suppose they were to be the first
two following 5. Then we might call: 7-4-5-
3-6. An almost certain method of concealing
them is to have your quarter invert them—
as the first two digits. Thus if we wanted 3
and 6 he would not call out 3-6-8, but

6-3-8. Or, if using double numbers, instead of calling 36-27-59 he would say, 63-48-51. On hearing 63 (the first double number called) the players would mentally invert it and derive 36, the play that the quarter wants them to play.

If opponents seem to have "caught on" that your odd numbers go to your left and vice versa, you might have your quarter *subtract one* from the signal. Thus, if he wanted 36 he would really call 35, to which his team mates would *add one,* making the desired play 36. The other team, hearing an odd number (35) would again assume it was going to your left. They would be a bit upset to observe the play unfolding to the right. The same purpose can be served by having your quarter *add one,* while the team silently subtracts it again; or by having him add or subtract 10 or 11 (for mystification purposes). This may sound a bit complicated, but it is, in reality, much easier to do than it sounds. I have done this scores of times with fairly inexperienced players and found no resultant difficulty whatever.

Of course it is well to keep the same key as long as possible; but sometimes one gets a "hunch" that the other team may have the signals and then he likes to know how to change them without changing the entire system, and yet "fogg up" the opposition.

In such a system as this the numbers from 20 to 30 would be assigned to all the running

plays that fell to the lot of the quarter back.
The numbers from 30 to 40 would belong, of
course, to the left half, those from 40 to 50
to the right half and those from 50 to 60 to
the full back. Numbers from 60 to 70 might
be saved up for trick plays, double passes,
plays to the short side, etc. Still another ten
numbers, from 70 to 80 might be devoted to
forward passes. This leaves 20 more for punts
or what not.

It is worth stating here that some teams
use signals that have no system to them whatever. Numbers are assigned to plays, as giv-
en out by the coach, in the most haphazard
and arbitrary manner imaginable. Here the
one number tells everything; and the theory
is that, being based on no system whatever,
it is undecipherable, because no number has
any systematic reference to any other number
and so it constitutes the "best system in the
world." Perhaps so.

## Charging Signal

This brings me to the matter of a charging
signal, which most coaches consider a very
important matter.

The most common method of using a hidden
or concealed charging signal is to have the
quarter call two different sets or series of
numbers. The first set tells who is to get the
ball and where he goes, as has been explained
above, including just when the ball is going

to go into play. Usually the ball goes into play at some particular stage in the calling off of the numbers of the second series, and that particular stage changes or varies automatically according to the instruction on this point contained in the first set of numbers called. For instance, if the first number of the first series is an odd number then the ball will be snapped back on the calling of the third number of the second series, but if that first number of the first series is an even number then the ball will come back on the second number of the second series. Or, if the first number of the first series is between 20 and 30 then the ball will go into play on the second number of the second series; if between 30 and 40 it will be the third number, and if between 40 and 50 it will be on the fourth number.

Suppose the last mentioned method is the one employed. Then the signaler might call something like 46-36-87-53. In this the first number, being between 40 and 50, would mean that the ball was going into play simultaneously with the calling of the fourth number of the second series. The second double number, 36, might be the signal for the particular play desired, while the other two numbers are surplusage.

Then ensues a slight pause, with every man of the offensive team set and listening for the quarter to start calling off his second series, which is often called in single digit sequence, no matter whether the first set was called in single

or double numbers. He calls clearly, smoothly
and with perfect rhythm something like 5-3-
9-4, and everyone of his team knows that when
the instant comes in that rhythmic cadence that
calls for the quarter to pronounce the fourth
digit, simultaneously with its pronouncement,
and not before nor yet after that pronouncement, the snapperback is going to send the
ball back, and, also simultaneously with that
fourth pronouncement and with that snapback, all four of the backs are going to start
at top speed and all seven of the linemen are
going to charge their hardest into the opposing line, on the certain assumption that the
ball will have gone back into action, even as
they went forward into action.

If the second series of numbers consists of
double numbers it is generally undertood that
the ball will come and the men will go simultaneously with the pronouncement of either
the first or the last digit thereof, as may be
agreed upon.

Oftimes it is understood that the ball is going to be snapped on the pronouncement of
the number following a particular other number, as 5, no matter where the quarter may
see fit to call 5 in the second series.

Sometimes teams are trained to charge just
the fractional part of a second ahead of the
pronouncement of the significant number in
the second series. This means, that they are
intentionally ' beating the ball,'' but so
slightly that it is difficult for the referee to

detect it. This, of course, is contrary to the
exhortations of the Rules Committee to be
found under the paragraph "Beating The
Ball" and found in "The Football Code" in
the front of every rule book.

If, however, players do not try to get off
*ahead* of the snapping of the ball but only
simultaneously *with* it, there can be no
doubt it is perfectly legitimate to use a concealed charging signal of this character, and
when well learned, and smoothly and evenly
executed, it is a good thing. By its use the
offensive team knows, or is supposed to know,
exactly when the ball is going to go into play,
and knowing this it seems clear that they can
spring into action at identically the *same*
instant that the ball does; whereas if they
waited till they saw the ball actually move it
is clear they would be leaping into action *after*
that snapback had started, and not along
*with* it. But the opposition team, not knowing when the ball is going to go into play, can
only go into action after they have seen their
opponents, the offensive team, make a starting or charging movement. This puts them
a trifle behind in the charge, and that trifle
should be sufficient to put them at a decided
disadvantage in their endeavors to break or
charge back the offensive rush line.

While theoretically this is correct reason-
ing, and so a vast majority of coaches will
agree, the writer is by no means thoroughly

convinced from his experience that it always works out that way.

Observe two roosters fighting. They point each other beak to beak. Then they spring up—*both* spring up—simultaneously—*always* simultaneously, at least so far as our human eyesight goes. No observer can ever tell which cock it was, on any particular spring, that decided to spring first, for the other cock psychologically guesses and gauges that intent so accurately that he finds no difficulty in speeding up his own spring so as to catch up with the other's, and the two leaps come absolutely together each time.

It will be replied that two football teams are not two fighting roosters. My answer is that when both teams want the game very badly and both are keyed to the highest possible pitch then, to all practical intents and charging purposes, they ARE two roosters, and that the one team will, other things being equal, charge as fast as the other, regardless of hidden snapping signals. They seem able to read the charging intent in the eye. Nay, I have proven this to my own satisfacttion in many a game and in many a season by having my snappers put the ball in play by simply having the quarter call out sharply and snappily the single word "Hike!", and on this command the backs start, the linemen charge and the snapper snaps the ball. True the other team then knows as quickly as does my own just when the ball goes into play; but my belief is that if my team is on edge that day and is a superior football team to the other it will win regardless of the other team knowing when the ball is going into play. At all events teams have won under such circumstances from the very best in the land, many a time and oft, with just that simple signal, and the very best teams I ever had used that same simple starting signal.

On the other hand I have nothing to say against the concealed starting signal and have also used it to excellent purpose numbers of times.

I might add that some teams include the starting signal right in the first series of numbers. This is done by including in the first double number called a digit of low degree like 2 or 3. The next double number, say, is the signal for the desired play. Then on the second or third (as the case may be) number after the pronouncement of the play signal the ball comes back. Of course this is perfectly possible, but the interval of time allowed for inexperienced players in which to interpret the play signal and to get and be ready for a hard charge so soon after hearing the play signal is decidedly short, and they had therefore better make two sets of numbers of it if they wish to use a concealed charging signal.

Of course if you have in your repertoire of plays quick shifts it is impossible to use them in conjunction with a hidden charging signal, because with quick shifts the ball must come and the players must charge *instantly* after the shifters have come to a complete stop. This interval of time, between the coming to a stop and starting again on their charge, should be uniform each time so they themselves will learn the rhythm of it, and it should be so short an interval that there would not be time for the calling of sets of numbers containing a hidden charging signal. Here the ball must come on a certain beat of the rhythmic movement of the shift or else on some sharp word of command like "Hike!" the instant the shifters have come to a stop after their shift.

One final word about concealed charging signals. For the team as a whole, such a system is only as good as its poorest performer. Now, if just one player of the offense gives away by the slightest premature look, gesture, movement or eye flash that the ball is, to his knowledge—or even if he is mistaken as to the exact instant of projected snapping— about to go into play, he will start *all* of the defensive team into charging action. The result will be that most of the offensive team (those that held firm and waited patiently for the charging instant) have really, and after all, *been outcharged* by the opposition. Some raggedness of execution is almost inevitable where a concealed signal is used, and perhaps that is why a plain "Hike" for everybody works out just as well in the end as something more intricate that is much more difficult to execute smoothly and with absolute unanimity.

b-bo bass

hand hand

## CHAPTER IX.

## KICK-OFF, ON SIDE KICK-OFF AND RE-CEIVING KICK-OFF.

Few teams put in as much practice on kicking-off and on receiving kick-offs as the subjects deserve. The individual that kicks the ball frequently does, perhaps, but his team does not go down under those kicks as often as it should in practice to enable the men to observe what a field really looks like with 22 widely scattered players running over it, most of them in different directions. No other stage of the game's progress looks like the kick-off.

But no coach can get time enough on the field to permit of giving the men prolonged practice on all, or even a half of the things that belong in the game; and if he could be given the men hours enough in the day they would be utterly exhausted long before he would be satisfied that they had had enough of what they needed. Accordingly he must or should figure out just what departments of play his men need most practice on, just how much work they can stand and just how much time he will allow for each; it's a daily compromise.

Everybody realizes that to kick a ball over the goal line at the opening of the game is a good start. True, if opponents do not elect to run it out again then and there,—and they usually don't so elect—it is a touchback and they are entitled to 20 yards from their own goal line. Had the kick remained in the field of play they would probably have been able to bring it back to the 25, 30 or even 40 yard line before being downed, and so, by comparison, you have done pretty well to restrain them to their 20 yard line, even though it was through the medium of a touchback kick-off.

How is it done? Largely it depends on the power of the kicker's leg swing. Much more than is ordinarily supposed it depends also on the accuracy and directness with which his toe and the impact of his kick met the end of the ball's long axis. Oftimes, too, there is a strong wind with him. And the rest depends on how the ball is teed up.

Often a player finds that though he cannot get the ball across the goal line he can get it down for 50 yards with pretty fair consistency, and that he can get good height to the kick as well. If he can do that it's almost as well as though he could send it across the goal line, for the height will give all of his men time to get down the field under it by the time it comes down, and they should be able to nail the receiver before he has brought it back very far.

Usually kickers tee the ball up high and pointing pretty straight up when they want to get them up in the air; but with some kickers it doesn't seem to make much difference how it is teed: it seems to depend a deal on knack. Most good kick-off men put their toe right against the end of the ball, but I have seen some good ones that sent it against the ball's side, with the lacing directed toward the goal posts; and then again I have seen some surprisingly long kicks registered by digging the toe under the ball and hitting its bulge with the instep.

## Lining the Team Up.

When all is ready for the kick-off the kicker should go back from the ball a distance of about 15 yards, while the remainder of the team line up five yards back of the ball. If the man that is to kick off is to remain behind as safety man the other ten will all go down field, and five should go on each side of the ball. They should divide the width of the field pretty evenly between them although the two ends will be nearer to their respective boundary lines than they will be to their next door neighbors, their tackles. In fact the ends should practically stand on or touching their boundary line. That means that with ten men spread out over a width of 160 feet with equal

spaces between them, there will be revealed
nine gaps of nearly 18 feet each. And coaches
will do well to accurately pace off this distance for each man several times during a
season and show their men just how wide a
hole 18 feet is. If you ask them to take that
distance apart from one another without
first stepping off the distance for them you
will be astounded to find how widely their
guesses vary. Let them have a look at the
real distance now and then and it may save a
disaster.

The next thing to bear in mind is that
it won't do to have all your fast men on one
side of the ball and none on the other, unless you are thinking of working some kind of
a trick. Possibly you figure on having your
kicker boot it down to one special corner, and
that by setting your fastest men opposite, or
in front of, that corner you will pin the receiver to a short come back. Probably you
might, if that receiver could be counted on to
bring it straight up the field; but he is just as
apt to bring it back in a swinging diagonal,
and if all your slow men are going down on
the side toward which he is coming no doubt
he'll make a good thing out of it.

Now we assume that the ends, on the extreme flanks, are fairly fast men. Then come
the tackles who are not so fast. Next should
come fast men again, and these are the halves.
Adjacent to them we station the slower guards
and then we wish we had two more real fast

men, and the best we can do are the full back
and the center, who ought to be fairly fast at
least. This arrangement would leave the
quarter to kick the ball; but if some other
player kicks off it is a simple matter to have
the quarter trade places with him for that
play.

Everybody is ready and each man is watching his kicker as he approaches the ball. Every man is tense and set to get off to a fast
start. What's the idea of having them five
yards back of the ball? So they will be off
with a flying start the instant they cross their
own 40 yard line, on which the ball is now re-
posing. You think they might be ahead of the
kicker at the instant he kicks? Not if they
have been watching him with care and do not
start until he reaches the line they are on—
the 35 yard mark, for he, having started 10
yards further back, has already attained his
flying start, and it should be a dandy. They
pick him up from a dead start, but they over-
come their dead start by the time they reach
the line of the ball.

Well, about the ends. They go down
straight—and fast of course—everybody as
fast as he can go save the one safety man
left behind, who looks out for a possible immediate return of the punt (by another punt)
and also he stays back away from the opposing blockers so that by no chance will he have
his legs cut out from under him, for if the
receiver should clear everybody else the safe-

ty man must still be right in his path at the
instant he seems to be breaking clear of the
field.

Yes, the ends have gone down hugging
their boundary line, and they should do so for
at least 20 yards, except under extraordinary
circumstances, and usually for a considerable
distance further. They should not be lured
into cutting toward the middle line of the field
because the ball has gone there — not for
awhile at least; nor should they be badgered
into taking the inside channel because an opponent is stubbornly blocking them in. If
necessary they should run out of bounds in
order to make sure of going down *on the
outside*. If they cut in they are most likely
to find the runner bringing the ball back
up their side of the field and to see him scamp-
er safely down the lane the end himself created
by leaving his reliable side line partner.

The remainder of the men run hard, watch
the receiver, keep in front of him, use their
hands vigorously to fend off blockers, *and*—
try to keep an eye on what is happening to
their own team mates on either side of them.
The idea is that they must all go down field
keeping relatively as near and as far from one
another as they were when they started. If
they do not keep uniform gaps between themselves the runner is going to "spot" an extra
big one, and the first thing you know he'll be
slashing through it for a touchdown from
kick-off. Look for a moment at this diagram,

in which I have indicated by lines from
the tackles what may happen if they violate
this principle.

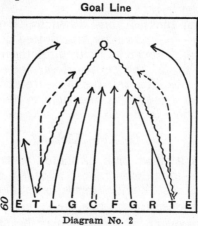

Diagram No. 2

Observe that the left tackle has gone down
too close to his left end, he has taken over
a part of the end's responsibility while shoving on his half back on his right, a part of
that which he should have kept for himself.
On the other side the case is just the reverse,
and quite as bad; the right tackle has cut in
sharply toward the middle, instead of going
down on a careful, outside, convex curve, as
the right end has properly done, and by so
doing he has created a gap between himself
and his end that the opposing runner romps
through. The right end cannot help this; he
is going down the way he has been instructed
to go. It is just such misplays as this that

cause touchdowns from kick-off to happen every now and then and scarcely anybody on the field understands how it happens. Simple enough, isn't it?

Had the tackles gone down as they should have run—as shown by the dotted lines—the runner could never have brought the ball back along either of the routes described by the waving lines, for the tackles would always have been exactly in position to tackle him had he tried to do so.

### The On-Side Kick-off.

This is a short kick, intended to travel but ten yards or a trifle more. Once it has gone that distance the kicking side has as much right to secure the ball as the receiving side.

This recovery of kick-off may be attempted by kicking the ball, which has been set quite upright, very near the top. This will cause it to roll over and over on the ground with a wobbling roll that travels slowly. The fastest men on the kicking team are placed on either side of it, to begin with, and they almost keep pace with it as it goes. The men standing in the front row for the defense are usually guards and a center—large and more or less slow men comparatively, unused to falling on the ball and to handling it cleanly. Besides, the kicking side has the advantage of numbers and of the surprise involved in such a kick-off.

Another way to pull an on-side kick-off is

to have a small man hold the ball, as one would for a try at goal following a touchdown, on the right hand side of the kicker. This he does every time his team kicks off in a game or two ahead of the important game in which the trick kick-off is to be tried, and he does it perhaps to start the game off even against the big team, to let opponents see that no unusual or dangerous thing whatever is happening; the kicker simply puts it far and high, as usual.

But when the defense has been lulled to sleep, and the next time comes when our tricksters are to kick-off, something curious does happen. Presumably all spectators, and all of the defensive team as well, are watching the supposed kicker as he advances on the ball from a position 15 yards back. When he gets within about 8 yards of the ball we see the first man on his left hand side leaving the 35 yard line and advancing diagonally toward the ball from the left. The kneeling quarterback twists the ball slightly around as this man advances on it, points it to suit, the advancing player on the left neatly puts his toe into it and the ball soars upward and diagonally forward, but more toward the right hand boundary line than down field. As his toe meets the ball the four fastest runners of the kicking side, grouped on that side purposely before the ball was kicked, shoot down under it like thunderbolts. The two fastest head right for that slow guard; perhaps three of them make him

their target.  What chance is there  for him?
Meantime the others are breaking their necks
for the ball.  If the kick has been practiced it is
not difficult to make.  It goes into the air not
too high yet high enough to give these fast men
time to travel ten   yards forward, and if they
get to the spot simultaneously with  it they are
four to one against that lone,  clumsy  guard,
wholly unused to catching punts as he is.

Immediately after the kick the man who was
far back and who usually makes the kick runs
to the right to back up the play.

## Receiving the Kick-off.

As the player kicking off for the offense will,
in a vast majority of times, essay to put the ball
as far down field as possible, the best  catchers
and returners of kicked balls on the defensive
side will be stationed the farthest  back to receive them.    These are usually the backs.

Quite a variety of  team  formations  to receive the kick-off have come to light in the last
dozen years.  In most of them  the  Center is
placed from 10 to 15 yards in front of the ball,
on a line by himself.  Usually the two guards
are placed out to the sides and on a line 5 yards
behind their center.  In some formations they
stand about 10 or 15 yards from the boundary
line, while in others they stand quite close to
the edge of the field.  So much depends on what
disposition is made of the tackles and ends back
of them. If the guards are close to the boundary

the tackles stand in much further.  If both the guard and the tackles are kept well away from the boundaries then the ends are placed close to the margins: somebody must be on hand to retrieve a ball that is sent far to one side of the field yet stays in the rectangle.

The quarterback, being fast and a sure catcher, is generally stationed where he may fairly be expected to find most of the kick-offs coming to him, and that is in the middle of the width of the field about 15 yeards in front of his own goal line.  Behind him are usually placed the full back, standing under the cross bar, and the halves far out toward either end of the 5 yard line, so that they with the full will be about equally distant from the point from which the ball is to be kicked.  That would look about like this:

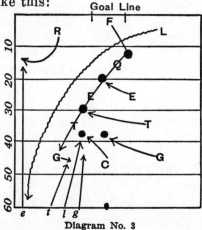

Diagram No. 3

Incidentally I have shown the system of interference for the ball to be brought back by,
say, the left half back, crossing to the opposite
side of the field. Similarly the right half could
cross to the left side. Note also how easy it
would be to assemble the ends, tackles and
guards so to form a lane, with three of them on
on each side, and have the runner bring the ball
straight up the middle and through this lane.
This is often done when the ball goes to the
quarter or the full back.

Not a few coaches believe that it is best for
the receiver of a kick-off, no matter who he is
or where he plays or catches the ball, to bring it
straight up the field from where he is after
making the catch. It must be admitted that
every inch of every step he takes in such case
is ground gained in the paying direction. Also
there can never, in such a system, be any doubt
in the mind of any of his team mates as to just
where he is going to come, and so where the
interferer ought to go to give him direct help.

Another receiving formation is one in which,
the center and guards would be on the front
line, all 15 yards back. Then would come the
tackles and the full back on another line 15
yards back of them. Then the ends and quarter
another 15 yards back, and then the two halves
last of all standing on the goal line. This I have
seen in use, but I do not think much of it.

In the formation diagrammed above we see

the right half being delegated to keep the end coming down on his side out of the play. In some line-ups the guard plays nearer the boundary than shown in the diagram and he attends to the defensive end coming down on that side. His job is to keep the end turned IN, in such a case, so that when the back with the ball comes up that side there will be a clear lane, free of adversaries, along that side line. The remainder of the team will then form a solid wall of blockers coming up the field on the left of the runner (L).

Presumably everybody is more or less familiar with the double pass play between the halves on receipt of kick-off. It can be played with most any receiving formation. Suppose, for instance, in the diagram shown above, the ball had gone to the right half, instead of to L. In that case R would have started to his left, while L was starting toward the right. As they passed each other R would simply pass the ball backward to L crossing the field behind him. The opposition would, if not on the lookout for the play, start down field inclining toward their right side, seeing that that was the side R was making for. The remainder of the receiving team would go straight up field a few steps and then swerve to their own right and come on substantially as shown in the diagram. The pass could, of course, be made between any two men.

About the commonest fault shown by teams is a bad tendency to go forward and engage the

oncoming tacklers long before the ball has come
down out of the clouds. They simply have not
the strong patience to wait a bit before they
start running forward. Their eagerness to get
into it is commendable; but they advance so
soon it simply means that by the time the ball
comes down into the hands of the receiver the
latter, after catching the ball, will look up to see
where his helpers are and will be dumb-
founded to find there are none in his
vicinity: they have all, apparently, de-
serted him. What they should have done
was to assemble in front of him. Then
they should have waited there till he had
caught the ball, had run forward a few steps
till he had about joined them and had called
"Go," before they were warranted in starting
*forward.* If they do not so assemble—more
or less back where the receiver is—it simply
means they are going forward as a scattered
field, and the kicking-team players find no difficulty whatever in sifting through that scattered field. The consequence is that several of
them are right down on the receiver almost before he can get out of his tracks—and there is
then not one of his teammates on hand to block
for him: They have all rushed on with empty
guns and left their ammunition wagon far behind them. Only persistent drilling will over-
come this serious fault in a team.

To the defensive center I wish to say one
word: If the kicked ball comes straight at you

don't try to catch it. You can't possibly do it. The thing is coming with too great velocity: it will rebound from your chest and the ball will be theirs. Step aside, when you see that kind coming, and let it go on through to the tackles.

If any player sees that the ball is coming down dead overhead, or a step behind him, he should not back up to take it. It is much better and easier for the player behind him to come forward and get it; and so the first man ought to ignore the ball, go forward and block for the man behind. This of course does not apply to the men stationed back last of all: they will have to take an overhead ball even if they have to run back to get it.

Centers and guards should always be on the sharp lookout for a possible short, on-side kick-off; and they should practice falling on ground balls, and also on catching short fly balls.

The receiver of a kick-off ought always to be on the lookout for the possibility of an opponent being diverted from his straight downfield course by some blocker, of the receiver's side, persistently driving the man to one side or the other. If the latter fails to get back into his own proper course there is sure to be a big wide lane between that diverted enemy and his next door neighbor from whose side he has wandered. That gap is the one the receiver should spot and take like a flash.

(See Diagram No. 2.)

Princeton took a formation recently, to receive kick-off, in which but two backs were in the rear row. This meant they had to divide the width of the field (160 feet) between them. Can it be successfully done? It was so done in that game. The idea is to get one extra interferer ahead of the runner. At the same time it almost ensures that one or other of the best two catchers and runners on the team will always receive the kick-off.

A low, driving kick, with a bit of wind behind it, would be pretty apt, I should say, to carry the ball between those two backs for a touchback before either of them could get behind it, like a line drive in baseball. The answer: don't take that formation against that kind of a kicker, and especially not with the wind blowing strongly in your face.

## CHAPTER X.

### OFFENSIVE FORMATIONS.

To most readers I fear my treatment of this subject will prove somewhat disappointing. They will expect a great deal, whereas space limits, as contemplated in this work, forbid my going into the subject deeper than just to my ankles.

In the good old days there was only one general offensive formation in the game and that was used by all teams. For many years all teams lined up, when they had the ball, as shown below:

Diagram No. 4

Now and then we still encounter a team using this simple looking formation, and I am very far from saying that it is not as good today as many another one we see in use. But, without more

174

ado, I will set down a number of widely differing formations that are in use today, or that the writer has seen employed by some team or other in recent years:

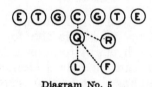

Diagram No. 5

This is a formation used with telling success by Cornell some years ago. Since then it has been adopted by many teams. Notice that the backs have a square formation. Some teams always hunt for a big, fast man to play the front half in the tandem on the right side of the square, and if the formation were shifted to the left the same man would still be front man in the tandem.

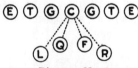

Diagram No. 6

Here is another formation used to considerable advantage by the University of Nebraska not so long ago. Observe how differently the backs are disposed in this formation from the preceding two.

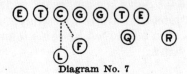

Diagram No. 7

This is about the way Pittsburgh lines up at
the present time.  This is the formation that
Coach Warner brought to such a fine stage of
perfection at the Carlisle Indian School and
with which he has since had such signal success
at Pitt.  I have shown the formation as it lines
up to the right; of course it can be taken on the
left side to equal advantage:

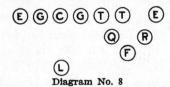

Diagram No. 8

The formation above is one lately employed
by Syracuse and exploited with telling success.
Of course it has some variations but the diagram
is substantially correct.

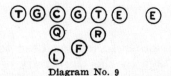

Diagram No. 9

Here is another in common use that has paid
good dividends:

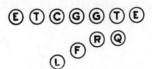

Diagram No. 10

And this is still another:

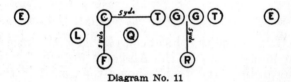

Diagram No. 11

The one shown above was used by the writer to excellent advantage one season when he had a team that only averaged 154 pounds in weight. This proved simply great for a light fast team. The formation can be taken both to right and left:

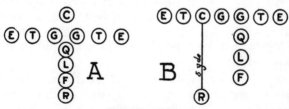

Diagram No. 12

In the above diagrams A shows the set of the Georgia Tech team several years ago before it had shifted, while B shows what the lineup

looked like after the shift and just before the
ball went into play.

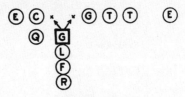

Diagram No. 13

Here is one that has been played with success
for many years by the Alabama Poly Inst.  In
the preliminary "set" shown the guard in the
square becomes the seventh man on the rush line
by jumping up to join the group of three linemen to the right, or else the other two to the
left, before the ball is put in play.

Diagram No. 14

Again, I have seen the backs arranged in the
above order.

It takes an experienced football man to be
able to see at a glance what each of the above
formations is good for.  Suffice it to say that all
these and many others have been worked and
labored with until their originators have proven
them possessed of possibilities no one could
have dreamed they had.

I have not the space to go into the least detail with any of them, and, of course, I cannot think of outlining the hundreds of plays that can be sprung from them all. On top of this we have to bear in mind that there are many varying punt formations, and also many widely differing "spread" or open formations. Of the latter a fair example is one in use by the Virginia Military Institute. They have been using it with distinct success. It follows:

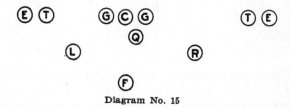

Diagram No. 15

Another spread formation that has proven popular with various teams is the following:

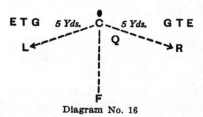

Diagram No. 16

And here follows a formation obviously constructed mainly for forward pass purposes:

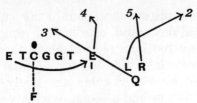

Diagram No. 17

Take a look at this freak:

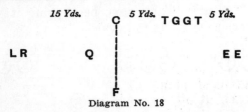

Diagram No. 18

Here the two ends on the right may jump up at the last second before the ball goes into play, making seven men on the line, with one end, the center and all three backs on the left eligible.

Or only one of the ends, and one of the backs, may jump up, and so change the status of eligible catchers altogether.

Or two of the backs on the left may jump up, making one of them eligible, leaving the one that stays back eligible, and making both ends and the right tackle eligible.

Or all three left hand backs and both ends on the right might be on the line of scrimmage before the ball is snapped, and then, just before it goes into play, any three of them could jump back a yard. Figure on that awhile.

The possibilities in the way of new and effective formations on the offense have by no means been exhausted.  In a large number nowadays we see involved the use of one back who takes advantage of the rule that permits one man of the offensive team to be in motion toward his own goal at the instant the ball goes into play.

The men who can with fair satisfaction coach high school, academy and minor college football teams are ten times as numerous as they were but a few years ago, and the average run of these do not need detailed diagrams of a full system of plays.  Hence the few that I will give are intended mainly for those teams that have no coach at all, or one whose experience has been very limited.  To such a team or coach a few general suggestions can be made with profit and these will apply to all formations. They follow:

The weakest spot in any defensive team's line-up is the gap between end and tackle.  Accordingly, your best energies on offense should be directed toward perfecting a heavy and reliable attack at that point.  This spot is the one assailed by the so-called off-tackle plays or short end runs.

This should be coupled with a good strong buck aiming between the opposing tackle and guard.  The idea is to keep the defensive tackle on the jump with plays that go inside of him alternated with attacks that go just outside of him.  The one play is a foil to the other, and if both are strong and dangerous it will keep that opposing tackle in hot water all the time figuring whether to play out wide or come in closer.

You must choose a formation that will permit of an attack being launched at any and every point of the defensive line. You must be prepared to assail the point of especial weakness in the opponents' line, no matter where it shows up.

Also you must take care to have in your backfield at least one good punter, at least one fine forward passer, at least one good bucker and, to be sure, at least two fast, flashy end and broken field runners. The more men you have there that can do all of these things the better; but it will not do to compose a backfield of four men none of whom can do well one of the things mentioned, no matter how well they all perform in the other three departments.

### End Running.

A quarter of a century ago the long end run, aiming to get all the way around opponents' end, was a play on which much time and coaching was expended. Gradually but steadily defense against this play improved until now it is rarely attempted in a game except from an open or punt formation, while not infrequently it is not even taught by coaches any longer.

Considered, however, as a freak or trick play it has its uses still, and if a team has the play in its repertoire and has the intelligence to produce it at a time when it can discern a way to get outside the defensive end and box him in, the play is as good as ever and stands to go for a fine sweeping gain.

I have previously adverted to the wide variety of offensive formations in use at the present time and to the vast number of plays that proceed from these, and so it will be best if I take a very simple formation by way of illustration, for I cannot discuss them all. Suffice it to say that in all there is the basic idea of so disposing the interference as to ensure protection for the runner on the inside by the linemen that come out for interference, while the free backs that are nearest to the opposing defensive end are the ones to look after him, no matter whether technically they are the other half, the quarter or the full, or whether their names are Jones or Smith. In other words, the assignment of what defensive players the interferers are to take off is a matter always of mere common sense.

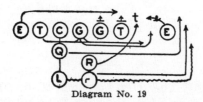

Diagram No. 19

In the above illustration I have shown the offensive end getting outside the defensive end and boxing the former in. To get there one may have a series of two plays on one signal, on the first play of which series (say, a buck or a forward pass) our right end overran the opposing end and remained outside of him in lining up for the second play of the series. This second play will be the long end run we are after and will be pulled off quickly without additional signal, in order that the defensive end may not discover that he is liable to be boxed in by an opponent who has cleverly taken up a position on his outside. If it has been impossible to get a man on the outside of the defensive end the offense will have to be content with trying out a shorter end run—one heading inside of opponents' end, which will be shown in the second diagram.

In the above diagram attention is drawn to the fact that all the backs run out straight for the boundary line, a distance of, say, 25 feet or more before thinking of turning down; otherwise they cannot hope to get clear around. It would be easy to explain why but would take too much space. Take my word for it, you *must* run so if the play is to be successful.

## Short End Run.

The short end run is much more effective against a good team than the long end run. If the halfback R can take off the defensive end by himself, or can hold him out for just an instant, L will have gone safely by into his hole.

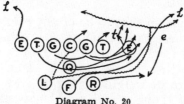

Diagram No. 20

In that case the second interferer (F) will not
have to help on E, but can go on and get the
opposing side back h.   But it must be admitted
that to take off an end single-handed calls for
a very good man and one of sturdy build.  If the
one man deputed cannot come through with the
assignment alone a second man (F) will have
to be delegated to help him out, for the defensive end *must* be put out of the play.

Note that our E, while boxing the tackle, also
does what he can to mess up opponents' loose
center or the backing-up full back coming along
to head off the play.

It will also be observed that I have both
guards and the far tackle coming around into
the play.  By some authorities this is considered dangerous; especially is it deemed risky
to pull the guard out on the side toward which
the play is going.  Observe, though, that I have
indicated for the left guard the duty of thrusting his elbow into the gap left vacant by our
right guard as the former comes running across;
and also I have shown the snapper charging so

as to block up that hole instantly after snapping the ball.

It is admitted that to be of any real use as interferers these three linemen that come out will have to be fairly speedy. The fact is that football is getting to be more a game of speed rather than of weight and physical strength. Celerity of thought and nimbleness of foot are the big things, and composite speed for the entire team is one of the chief assets we must seek to incorporate. True, all backs are supposed to have speed, but if we can also compose a rush line of men who have speed, and the coach knows how to utilize that speed, it becomes a mighty difficult undertaking to check such a team for sixty minutes of play.

Of course, if a coach hasn't linemen of any speed whatever he cannot hope to get line interference into his end runs but, by the same token, he cannot hope to make, in these days, much ground through the medium of end runs, either long or short, unless he has some line interference to help out his backs.

The runner on a short end run, say, to the right, after being convoyed safely to and through the line of scrimmage, should not, as a rule, continue on in his straight couse, but should either whip back instantly toward the left or else flick out sharply to the right. Either way he will do better than to continue on in a direct course.

A few teams still play to advantage the old-time quick-opening buck, in which a quarterback feeds the ball with extreme celerity to a halfback, who plunges straight ahead, either inside or outside of the tackle on his own side, with such nimbleness and speed that he gets through for good gains without any other assistance than what his linemen in front of him can give in opening up holes for him.

Also, quarterbacks from a position close up, still plunge unassisted for short gains straight ahead.

But nearly all fullback bucking calls for one, two or three other backs to go ahead and blaze the way. These interferers knife and crowd their way through to take off the secondary defense men, or else to help their linemen take out of the way a particularly difficult opponent in the line. But seldom or never do any linemen from another part of the line come back out of their positions in order to help make an opening in some other part of the line when the play is a genuine buck. It can't be done with safety; and so linemen on such plays stay where they are and turn their own direct opponent away from the play, thereby preventing him from telescoping the whole line by a powerful diagonal charge.

A coach should study long and hard over every play he uses with a view to determining just which linemen, if any, he can safely instruct to go through the opposing line without

delay and pick off the secondary defense men.
But he must never let his linemen attempt to do
this unless and until all dangerous men in the
primary line of defense are safely cared for
first, and this applies as well to end running as
to bucking. It might as well be said here that
a mere helter skelter rush of men at a given
spot will never yield satisfactory results. Each
man on every play must be sent against some
particular man on the defense and he must get
that man, else the play will or should fail.

### A Cross Buck.

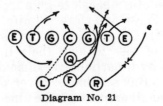

Diagram No. 21

This shows a halfback bucking; but inasmuch as the fulback is usually the best bucker
on a team, while halves are generally saved
for end running, a different formation would
be better for a fullback buck. Such an one
would be the following:

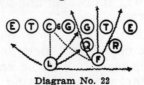

Diagram No. 22

This would also be good wherewith to send L around right end.  Or the snap to L could be held, by L delaying, till all three of the other backs ran across to the short side in interference for him, when he would fall in behind them and buck between his own left end and left tackle.  Of course F could go back to L's position to do his main bucking if so desired. The waving lines show the different lines of attack.

With this formation also all backs would be in good position for L to hurl forward passes. Again a nice double pass could easily be worked by snapping the ball to L who would head in for the hole between his own right end and right tackle and then pass the ball back to R, who would go around left end with the other two backs for interference.

This formation of the backs and these plays may be used either with a balanced line—three men on each side of the snapper—or with an unbalanced line—four on one side and two on the other.  Attention may also be drawn to the great number of points in the line that can be assaulted by the player F on getting the ball by direct snap.

## Unbalanced Formation.

Some coaches, in planning an unbalanced line attack, place the two guards on the long side, shoulder to shoulder.  This leaves a tackle and

an end on the short side. Some prefer to have
the two tackles on the long side leaving one
guard and one end on the short side. Still
others want the two ends on the long side, leaving a guard and a tackle on the short side; I
have even seen both ends on the short side,
which means, that both tackles and both
guards, with that team, are always found together on the long side.

Still other coaches try to determine which of
their men are best suited for long side play and
which are best for short side play, and always
station them according to their talents, regardless of whether the formation is to the right or
to the left and regardless of what positions they
are said to be playing in the line up. For instance, Smith, given out to the newspaper men
as right tackle, is found throughout
the game not only at right tackle when
the formation is to the right, but is likewise at left tackle when the formation
is to the left. Thus his duties are always uniform, no matter what the formation—and the
same way with Jones who always plays, say,
next to the snapper on the short side of the line.
There is considerable sense in this way of lining
up one's linemen.

The foundation of all offensives from close, unbalanced formation is, and must be, the attack
through the strong side of the line; and the
crux of that situation is the opposing tackle.

Accordingly all teams strive to develop a strong
off-tackle smash and a strong buck inside of
that tackle. Now with the same set of the for-
wards—four on one side of the ball and two on
the other, and with practically  the same arrangement of four  backs behind  the line  of
scrimmage, it is singular how differently different teams plan the assignment of work in blocking and interfering against the defensive players on just these two plays. What's more, most of
them seem to work out well, given good, spirit-
ed, well-drilled players to execute them.  Consider,  for  instance,  the  following  as  a
fair  sample  of  unbalanced  lineup; in
which  G,  T and  E  represent  the  right
guard, right tackle and right end respectively,
while X, Y and  Z represent  the left  guard,
tackle and end respectively; with *a, b* and *z*
(small) representing the defensive guard, tackle and end on the short side; C is the defensive
center and S the offensive snapperback.

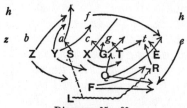

Diagram No. 23

Note that there is a small gap between T and
E, and frequently such a gap is left between the
tackle and end on the short side as well. If the

opposing tackle plays *in* that gap he is much
more easily "scissored" by T and E, while if
he play *outside* of E he is then so far out
that it should be easy to turn him out for a
flashing buck inside of him. The remainder of
the rush line, of course, play "tight line."

Now about R: I have arbitrarily placed him
squarely behind E, but merely for the purpose
of the more handily illustrating the varying
treatments of these two basic plays—off-tackle
smash and cross buck inside of tackle. Nearly
all teams play him either in closer or else out
farther, either behind the gap or outside his
own end. It depends so much on what kind of
plays you have in your repertoire. For some
of them no doubt it would be best to have R in
close, while for others it would be better to
have him out wide. But the general idea of
his duties can be well shown where I have stationed him.

The play under consideration is the short end
run (off-tackle smash), going between opposing
end and tackle. The arrow lines radiating from
the different players of the offense indicate the
different routes or duties that may be assigned
to them, according to the particular way the
coach plans this play. It will be observed that
E and R have only one direction line each,
which means that both of them are to work on
T and turn him in. L, who carries the ball, also
has but one line, and that is his running course.
S also has but one line, and it indicates it is his

duty to turn the opposing short-side guard away from the play and then, if possible, go through and block off the short-side half.

But all the remaining offensive players have MORE than one line, and this means that different teams pull this play off differently, with respect to such men at least. Study for instance, the lines of Q and F. Under some systems Q is designated to keep out *e,* and this would mean that F should go forward, as shown in his upper arrow line and get *f.* Under other systems F would take *e* out while Q would go forward without delay to get *f.* Against a very strong end it is likely both Q and F would be instructed to proceed against *e.*

Next note that T is shown with a choice of either boxing *g* in or of turning *t* out. If he does the former Q is free to decide between going after *f* or after *e;* but if T is to take *t* out then *g* is certain to come through the hole left open by reason of T charging toward the open, and in that case Q will have to go straight ahead and block *g,* in which case F would have to get *e* alone. This statement may be qualified to the extent of remembering that under some systems, in such case, R would charge in behind T and block *g,* while Q would still go on diagonally forward and take *f.* Looking now at G we see that he may be instructed to help T on *g,* or he may be told to go for the opposing *c.* It largely depends on whether T can handle *g* alone; also on how much trouble *c* is giving in the way of coming through into the backfield (in case X is leaving his position to swing into backfield interference). Perhaps c is not even playing on the line of scrimmage. In that case, if S, after snapping the ball, can keep "a" turned to his left there is no reason why X should not shoot straight ahead through the gap, as there will be no one in front of him, and then cut down c from the side. If T is an extra good man, and g is a rather weak player, it is often possible for T, with the side-swiping advantage he has, to block g in single-handed, and this would let G cross-check behind T.

Now study Y: If X is going to come back of his line in order to get into the interference then it is well to have Y come back also and, running close behind S, shoot his left elbow into the hole left by X coming out, in order that no charging opponent may unexpectedly come bursting through into your backyard. Doing this as he goes, he should now continue on his course and, if he is a fast and willing runner, he frequently overtakes a slow guard (X) and, passing him, does more "bloody execution" than his guard (who might better have gone through, in such case). Some coaches will not have a lineman come back in interference under any circumstances. Mr. Stagg and Mr. Bankart are said to be convinced it is better to send them through the line, and no one will deny the weight of the voices of these two highly successful coaches.

If Y is to go through the line he has a choice of going inside the opposing short side guard, a, or of going through outside of him. That will depend largely on just where a is playing, and also on how S is taking him. It's all again a matter of common sense. Similarly we can figure either that Z should go through in front, or else come back. In the former case he cuts over to the right to meet the play in front, cutting down f if he gets a chance. Should the runner get cut loose for a long run down the right side of the field Z should go on down the field and get the safety man. But if he expects L to whip back to the left, after getting through the line, of course he should take care of the opposing right back.

Thus we see it all depends on just how you expect to pull off the play; and that should depend somewhat at least on how strong or weak the various individuals are in the opposing defensive set, especially when studied in connection with consideration of just how your own men stack up in speed and in blocking calibre.

## The Buck Inside of Tackle.

It may profitably be pointed out here that the time to call for this off-tackle smash is when the opposing tackle is playing in too close and hence can easily be boxed in by the end and half. But if a few good gains are made thereby it will not be long before you will find the op-

posing tackle moving out wider. If, now, your
end and half have been lining up just about as
usual, always the same distance from their
own tackle, they will find themselves more or
less inside that opposing tackle, and so in good
position to turn him **out**. At such a time the
quarter should signal for the buck inside.

I will now show how one team concentrates
on this tackle for this buck:

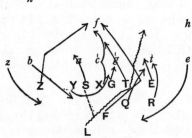

Diagram No. 24

On the assumption that the opposing tackle,
*t,* will not be lured out very far and that our
E will have to content himself with playing
squarely in front of him, we have so stationed
him. Then we note that E, R and Q have all
piled on him—E holding him up, if possible,
until Q and R can come up and help out. Even
F is shown going straight at *t,* and indeed he
also hits *t* if it seems necessary. This alone
shows how all important it is to *thoroughly*
dispose of *t*: the *near* danger in football must
*always* be effectively cared for, regardless of

what other perils and difficulties may loom up at a later stage of the play or the game. As F plows in he should note whether he is needed on *t*. If not he goes on through and takes *f*.

Under other systems T would take *t* out on this play, while either E, R or Q would help G turn *g* *in* and away from the play. So much depends on whether T is able by himself to turn *t* out. If he is, and *one* of the backs is sufficient to help G on *g,* then there would be a surplusage of backfield help to go on through and get *f* clean.

In any case L should buck in *straight lines* —no curving-out run, as in the case of an end run. If he does not go like an arrow for his hole— on the inside of F, he will surely run himself into *e.* Also he will have to go fast, else *b* will get him.

There are plenty of other assignments of interference used to open up on this buck, and many little points of detail as to how the linemen must work with each other to enable one or more of them to be spared from the immediate exigencies of line checking and go through at once to get the secondary, but these cannot easily be explained or taught except by actual demonstration on the field.

Much simpler in design are the bucks that are brought in nearer to the snapper, whether the ball is carried by L or F. Some will ask at once whether the rear back ought not always to be the man to carry the ball, inasmuch as this would always provide more free men ahead of him to help force a hole. The answers to this point are:

1. If the ball were always to be snapped to the rear man in your stock formation the defense would soon learn to concentrate their whole attention on that rear man, regardless of whether it was Jones this time and Smith the next. They must be kept more or less in doubt as to the direction and distance of the snap and the back to whom it is going.

2. It is not always the number of interferers in front of a runner or plunger that ensures success in a given play. Too many of them may choke up a hole, and at times they get in each other's way. Especially is this true if the prospective bucker is already close to the line, as is F in this formation. Being close it is about as well, generally speaking, to trust him to get to his opening quickly and shoot through for a good gain by virtue of his starting and knifing ability, and not always depend on interference to pave the way for him.

3. It should be remembered that F is or should be a heavy strong chap of good interfering ability and able to assimilate punishment: that's why he is placed ahead of L (or R) in the formation. To bring him back always in the position of rear man in order to get the ball would be to "put the cart before the horse," for obviously L and R are not built to do for him what he is asked to do for them. And yet F

must be asked to do his full share of the work; L and R ought not to be expected to carry the ball all the time. Accordingly it must at times be snapped to F, and it must be snapped to him in his regular position. One good man ahead of a quick bucker, to split the opening, is usually enough.

Coming to a consideration of modern plays that are hurled at the short side we note in the formation, that there is apt to be quite a gap between $a$ and $b$ on the defensive short side. This hole is practically not to be avoided by the defense—if Z will play a bit wide. Naturally, coaches and quarterbacks pick on this inviting "barn door." If a quarter is used to handle the ball from snapper he usually has a play in which he feeds the ball to L for a lightning-like thrust straight at this gap. Or he fakes to give the ball to L for a cross buck to the strong side and then gives it to F instead for a "split" buck to the short side. Or he gives it directly to F for a buck to the same place, and L, going forward side by side with F, keeps the opposing short end out of the play. As a rule no line man from the strong side is brought into the interference in these plays because they are begun and over with, either for a gain or no gain, before the linemen could get around. The same holds true of Q and R—they are too far away from the scene of action.

But all coaches ponder and puzzle over this very situation. They are all looking for a new play to the short that will "crucify" the defense.  To make an assault in this vicinity as powerful as one to the strong side they realize the play must have the man-power that plays to the strong side have, and the big question is how one is to get that man-power assembled in that narrow corner and, once there, how the men are all to be assigned worth-while duties without so interfering with each other as to clutter everything up.

Many teams know of no better answer to this situation than the double-pass reverse play; and it is to be doubted whether any better answer has been found by anybody.  It certainly has stood the test of time and has worn quite as well as any intricate play ever devised.  Coach Warner, of Pittburgh, must be given credit for the highest form of development of this play, and though details of execution are beginning to differ under different coaches, its general principles are fairly illustrated in the diagram below:

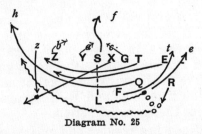

Diagram No. 25

To coach Bezdek, of Penn State, is given cred-

it for the basic idea involved in the following
short side play:

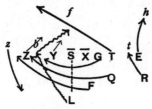

Diagram No. 26

After receiving the ball from the snapper,
L must delay an instant or two until his interference can get across to the short side. They
sweep across, in front of him, while he, standing
still in his position, raises the ball aloft   as
though to forward pass it. This causes the defense to hesitate perceptibly in its charge and
holds the secondary men back, whereas they
should be coming up fast to tackle.   L pulls the
ball back down almost instantly, tucks it under
his arm, falls in rapidly behind his interference
and smashes in. The play is being widely cop-
ied.

Pass-out plays  to the short  side have  been
tried in large numbers, but as a rule they do not
work out well: defensive half backs watch such
stunts mighty closely these days.

The reader will find some forward  passing
plays outlined in the chapter on Forward Passing.

## About Trick Plays.

So many coaches of minor teams write me asking for "a good trick play or two." Now, a really good trick play is a deucedly handy thing to have in one's grab bag, but the downright truth of it is that trick plays that will really work in this day and age are almost as scarce as "hen's teeth," and quite as hard to pull.

This was not always the case. In the early days of the game before offensive tactics had broadened out the way they now have, and before coaches had put in a life-time of study on ways and means to stop a varied offense, most any simple kind of trick—anything new—would no only work but work well. All the older coaches have invented scores of them in their time, but nearly all of them have worn out and been scrapped. Others have been legislated out of existence. Still others are no longer possible because the nature of the game has changed, and because the way team defense now sets—wholly apart from the question of improved individual defensive alertness—the trick would no longer work.

Once we used to have, when near the boundary line, double passes between the halves, the ball finally going toward the boundary and thence down the boundary line for long runs. No side line half would let a thing like that get by him in these days: it would cost him his job on the spot.

Or, when very close to the boundary, we had the play of the snapper hiding the ball under his crotch, with fake interference scurrying out to the open field. Then the boundary end, after a delay, took the ball from the snapper and *walked* on down the field to touchdown. The rules now decree that the snapper may not so hold the ball even momentarily. The trick has been "legislated out."

What about the famous old "on-side" quarterback kick? Well, you see, when the forward pass made its debut in polite society the defense soon found that to check forward passing they would have to station the halves at the exact spots where the quarterback kick used to go; and so those halves now not only keep a lookout for passes in their vicinity but they are, at the same time, "bull dogs and death" to most on-side kicks.

True, the double pass still lives; but not because it is any longer a "trick" play: it survives by virtue of the way it has been built up and developed as a practical, powerful, interference play.

Hiding the ball under the jersey and using the headgear to simulate the ball and so fool the opposition have both been legislated out. Likewise hiding on the side lines. Double passes through center wouldn't fool a screech owl under a midday sun. And so it goes.

The nearest things to  trick plays in  these days are the so-called "hidden ball" plays, in which the quarter (where one is used as an intermediate handler of the ball) fakes to give the ball to one man then, in reality, gives it to another or else keeps it.  Harvard has a good line of these.  Another wide field for mystification on offense lies in forward passing.  Here trickiness is not of the same nature as that of former days, but it is deception just the same.  As a matter of fact, we have  to-day  to rely very largely on the forward passing department to furnish opportunity to spring a new trick.

Some trick wizardry is possible for teams that employ quick shifts.  Under  cover of a kaleidoscopic movement it is easier to devise and spring something that will puzzle  opponents than with a stationary formation.   Penn State "fools 'em" every now and then  with such tid-bits.

Quick line-ups (Sequence or "series plays,) have been revived a bit of late.  They are not as practicable as years ago, for modern defense is ever on the lookout for them.  Besides, the introduction of  the forward  pass operates  to make them unserviceable because to include a pass in such a series is altogether too radical an attempt to compel oil and water to mix; yet the chances are excellent that you will want to employ some kind of a pass before  the series is played through, and then you will have to interrupt it in order to insert the pass: so why have a series that is so liable to interruption?

The idea of their use is to line up so fast as to get the ball off on the next play before the defense has realized the rapidity with which the offense is lining up and so will be found unprepared to meet these quckly renewed assaults. But modern defensive teams are usually ready.

If you must have a series I will explain that one usually consists of two, three, four or five plays—never more. The idea of their arrangement is to have several plays hitting at one spot, or going in the same direction, till you get the defense assembling and concentrating forces at that spot, then to suddenly shoot something that looks like a renewed attack at that same spot, which play, however, winds up as an assault at some other place defense against which has been weakened by the need of reinforcing the point that has been under heavy fire.

## General Pointers on Offense.

No team should have more than twenty offensive plays or forty signals. A team cannot have or keep them all in a high state of polish, and some of them will never be pulled off in a game anyway. In a game of average length the winning team seldom executes more than eighty plays, which means that with even forty signals each would be used, on the average, but twice in the game.

No play should be relied upon or used in a game unless and until it has been thoroughly learned and has received 100 per cent of polish

No offense can be considered well rounded or dependable that cannot show strength in all four departments—end running, line bucking, forward passing and punting. Therefore, do not neglect any of them.

All plays should proceed and develop from as few differing formations as possible. As the total number of plays a team can learn and perfect is limited, the greater the number of formations from which these are sprung the less must be the number of plays that can be learned from each different formation. And this means that it will be easier for opponents to diagnose what is coming when they know you confine yourself to but certain plays in certain formations.

No play can be considered a good one unless every player on the team has a specific duty—something to do that will aid the runner in his effort to gain ground.

1. Flanker right grab pass

## CHAPTER XI.

## PUNTING, PUNT FORMATION, RUNNING BACK PUNTS, PLACE AND DROP KICKING FOR GOAL, THE QUICK KICK, RUNNING BACK FROM PUNT, ETC.

"Poets are born, not made." That's about the way it is with punters. Ever to punt well one must be born with good coordination of hand and foot and eye. If a fellow hasn't the necessary looseness in his hip joint, if he hasn't a strong elastic leg swing, if he cannot time the dropping of the ball correctly to the upward and forward swing of his leg, if he can't locate the exact whereabouts of the ball with such accuracy that when his foot meets it he transmits to the ball, through that sledgehammer foot, close to 100 per cent of the energy generated by that powerful leg swing, what's the use of filling pages on pages of explanation to such an one as to how one becomes a fine punter?

A player who has downright talent for punting does all these things pretty well to start with—just naturally, in the same way that some other chap just naturally beats the rest of the gang in a short sprint or in hitting a pitched ball. However, there are some hints that can be given to such a man that may improve his kicking a bit and help him to get more height or more distance or more speed, or whatever it is he specially needs to make him a still more valuable "member of society."

Presumably everybody who knows anything at all about punting knows it is not done with the toe, but with the instep. Drop and place kicking usually are performed with the toe, but not punting.

If a man is a right-footed kicker the ball should be snapped to him slightly on his right and about chest high. He should step toward the right, in getting his swing, and he should rapidly adjust the ball in his hands while so stepping: he will not have time to adjust the ball first and then step, as some inexperienced men do, else, when he gets into college ball, he will find the opposing rush lines coming through so fast to block his punt that he will not have time to get rid of it before they are upon him. For the same reason he must learn to stand back at least 10 yards from the scrimmage line when he is really going to punt, and it will be even safer it he makes it 12 yards, which will allow him, then, two yards to advance, and he will still be back 10 yards at the instant the ball leaves his foot. That distance ought to make the whole proposition perfectly safe for him.

After catching the snap, three steps diagonally to the right and forward are all he can allow himself, else he will be running himself into that oncoming enemy rush line in spite of his distance back. This assumes that he wants to stride out first with his left foot, following which comes his right foot, and then his left again—three steps. But some good kickers manage to get up all the momentum they require by stepping out with the right foot first, then with the left and—BANG! goes the right foot into it—only two steps, you see. It's decidedly awkward for a man who has formed the habit of taking three steps to change his style to the two-step, but it certainly does save one from getting many a kick blocked.

Kickers that get a side swing into their kicking have, as a rule, more force in that swing than a man who swings his leg straight forward. The former get the torso into it and behind it, while the latter kick with the leg only and no part of the body behind the leg swing. Besides, the latter are more apt to have their kicks blocked.

Most spirals are produced by dropping the ball so it will be struck slightly on the outside of the instep. They bore through the air a bit further than non-spirals, but are generally easier to catch than the "floaters" that drift in all sorts of ways as they come down.

A punter should practice getting a good

height as well as good distance to his punts, else his ends will not be able to get down under them in time to nail the defensive catcher. It is generally conceded that a punter that gets great distance with insufficient height to his punt is not so valuable to his team as one that can only average from 40 to 45 yards but who gets them up into the air high enough to permit of his ends covering them.

Often a team has neither the one kind nor the other and the coach is at his wit's end to know what to do to bolster up his booting department. In such case he should look around for a back who can place the ball and put drive into his kick, even if he cannot put it up in the air nor give it distance on the fly. If he cannot unearth a man who will study the position of the defensive backs, and who can get rid of the ball with a fair degree of force, and place it where the opposition safety man is not, fairly satisfactory results can be derived from a few days of hard work with such a kicker. If he can't kick them high but can kick low he should practice aiming them for some part of the field where there is no one set to catch them. The ball hits the ground and bounds along well to one side of the safety man. Of what advantage then is that safety man's catching ability? Has he practiced fielding ground punts? He has not. Does he know any better than anyone else how the ball is going to bound? He does not. Can he be depended upon to handle it cleanly? He cannot.  Half the time he is afraid to touch it at all till it all but comes to rest, and by that time the kicker's ends are upon him and he doesn't bring it back a yard: he's lucky to even have it.  And generally such a kick has gone close to the boundary line and his team will be handicapped to work offensively with it, for a few downs at least.

And such a kicker can often  put it  out of bounds at opponents' five yard line.  That is where it should be kicked whenever possible, instead of across their goal line.  By the way, why do otherwise perfect kickers so often boot the thing clear across for a touchback anyway? How is it they so seldom understand that there are times when it is a short kick, not a long one, that is wanted?   I tell my own punters  all about it, and they nod and say they understand perfectly.  Then comes the game, and, sooner or later, I see my team held for downs on, say, opponents' 30 yard line.  I see my punter drop back, which puts him 40 yards from that goal line.  I say to myself:  "This time he will remember.  He will kick  it high, but  not far. When it comes down it will bound up and down between their goal and their 10 yard line and they will have to play with it at that spot— under the shadow of their goal posts.  How clever I am to have remembered  to tell him that."

And then the ball comes back, my  punter catches it, his foot swings into it and—"Merciful heavens!—the idiot has belted it *again* clear beyond the end zone." A beautiful punt, yes, but not the kind we want at this point. I know all coaches have similiar experiences. Frankly, I don't know how to stop them from doing it. They cannot seem to get it in their heads that if a team has at times need of short forward passes, as well as of long ones, it should, at times have need of short punts as well as long ones?

One word more: if the ball is off to one side, close to the boundary, the punter must take care on the one hand that he does not drive it out of bounds before it has travelled more than 15 or 20 yards; and on the other hand he should bear in mind the danger of sending it too far out toward the open side of the field. It's hard to back up the latter kind of a punt—there is no one of your own team save one end out there to start off with, whereas the safety man of the opposition has been coached to play out there just for such an eventuality. Your open-side end is the one man that is being depended on to get him, and if he misses that opposing back is liable to bring it all the way back for a touchdown.

## Punt Formation.

For some years there has been a strong tendency to expend more and more time and thought on the Punt Formation. Every now and then some team, in working this old mine, stumbles on a new vein that pans out surprisingly well in pay ore, not alone by way of new forward passes but also new combinations of players that result in highly successful  end running and line bucking.

Some coaches prefer a balanced line for punting  and some an unbalanced line.  Most of the usual plays that proceed from the general formation may be played as well with the one as the other. Here is presented a diagram of the former, together with detail of a punt:

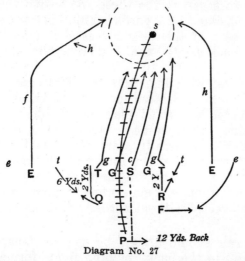

Diagram No. 27

The ends leave their tackles and go out anywhere from 3 to 10 yards, according to the plan of the particular coach.    But if they  go out there for a real punt then they must do likewise when the play, from punt formation, is to be a buck, an end run or a pass: that stands to reason. For a punt they are set to go down in a straight line the instant the ball is snapped. The arrow lines show the direction the men go, and whom they take. Note that the linemen going down have formed a corral surrounding the catcher. If each man does his work properly it will be impossible for the runner to escape.

The five center men converge in their charge so as to scoop in the three defensive center trio. Q, standing 2 yards behind his left tackle, takes care of their right tackle, R (same distance back as Q) handles their left tackle, and F looks out for their left end. As our punter is kicking with his right foot their right end needs no special attention. If our kicker were left footed we would place our tandem on his left side. Because he is right footed, our left tackle may generally start down field a trifle sooner than the other four close linemen, all of whom must wait till they hear the sound of the kick, though some centers manage to guess this correctly without actually waiting to hear it.

Spirals should always be used in snapping the ball to the back man on punt formation, whether it is a punt or an end run. Assuming the pass is good there is no reason why a punter should not have plenty of time to get it off. $1\frac{3}{4}$ seconds from the snapping of the ball is very fast work, but 2¼ seconds elapsed time would be fatally slow.

Assuming also that the backs all 'get'' their proper and respective men, the main reason why kicks are blocked is because the offensive linemen are too eager to get down the field and do something showy in the open. It's a meritorious ambition all right; but if it runs away with a lineman to the extent that he runs away from his primary duty it's going to spell disaster to his punter and his team. If, for instance, the left tackle starts down field without even touching the opposing right guard that man is coming right through on the lone quarter we have set on the left side; but Q is already busy stopping their right tackle: he can't stop both of them; and so one of them will most likely block the punt. Be a bit careful about that, you over-eager left tackles.

And what are the men on defense doing all this time? Well, if the ball is down inside their opponents' 20 yard line they will likely throw an extra man from the secondary up on the rush line, in a desperate endeavor to block the punt. If they succeed in so doing there is every likelihood that they will not  merely recover  the blocked punt, but that they will score a touchdown then and there. This makes it well worth while to run some risk regarding the possibility of the offense making a good running gain around their end or through the line because of this eighth man being on the line.  To be sure the offense, noting that there are few men in the secondary defense, and those drawn rather far back, may decide to do the unusual thing of dropping a forward pass over the rush lines; but it's worth the risk if the ball is that close to the opposition goal line. However, it is altogether too risky to put, say, nine men on the rush line, for that would practically leave nobody in the secondary defense.

The first thing a defensive rush line should do when opponents take punt formation, is to try to determine whether it is really going to be a punt or something else. In this they will have to be guided in large degree by a recollection of what down it is and what distance opponents have to gain. If less than fourth down and less than 2 yds to gain they are pretty apt to buck; or if between 2 and 5 to gain they may try an end run, in the middle zone. But deep in your territory with that much to gain, they are likely to attempt a pass, even though it is  last down; while if deep in their own territory, with that much to  gain, they are more than apt to punt even though it is but second down. And so it goes.

Assuming that they are going to punt, the primary duty of the lineman is to try to block that punt. But if a team has its punting game so well polished that there exists little  or no hope of being able to block the punt then the defense often concentrates on doing the next best thing—preventing their linemen from getting

down field quickly under the punt. Some
coaches, for instance, when the ball is between
the two 30 or 35 yard lines, with a punt sure to
be ordered, instruct their five center men on defense to literally tackle the opposing five center men, with the idea of preventing any of
them from getting down field. They tell their
end to rush in and hurry the punt, and they
draw their side backs back 15 yards and, as
soon as the ball is actually punted, these side
backs rapidly retreat still further. This results
in three free interferers being grouped in front
of the catcher. They have decided in advance
which side of the field they are going to tra-
verse in bringing it back, and so they practically ignore the opposition end coming down on
the other side, while all three free backs concentrate on getting rid of the one dangerous
man, the end, that is coming down on the side
toward which they are planning to go.

For years past much coaching and practice
have been expended on all fields teaching ends
and halves how to check and block opposing
ends coming down under punts. The most
usual method was for the defensive end (when
not trying to block the punt) to delay him as
much as possible at or close to the scrimmage
line. When he finally got by, the half took a
crack at him, and by that time the end was
on him again. Their masterstroke was to "clip"
him from behind just as he was about to tackle
their receiver. Clipping, however, has now

been ruled out, so that henceforth they will have
to get the end either from the side or in front.

The safety man should not ever take his eyes
off the punted ball in order to get the "lay of
the land:" that's how he comes to fumble and
bobble.  His big job is to get that ball, and as
it is about to land in his arms his companion
back should coach him which way to go, provided that point has not already been decided
upon between them in advance of the punt.

### Place and Drop Kicking.

If a field general wants a place kick formation there is no reason  in the world  why he
shouldn't call for it.  The fact that the defensive team hears the call doesn't mean that he
must actually try either a place kick for goal,
or drop kick any more than he must try a forward pass, an end run, a trick or anything else.

They will see the formation when it is taken
anyway, so why not call it out?

For either a place kick or a drop  kick for
goal the line lines up in perfect balance—three
men on each side of the snapper, with the ends
in close to the tackles, each man set low and intent on one thing only—blocking off the opponents as long as they possibly can, so giving
their kicker all possible time to get his kick off
safely.

If it is to be a drop kick there will be a tandem of two men on the right while only one man

takes station on the left.  The drop kicker goes
back whatever distance he desires, but this is
usually under 10 yards  rather than over. He
selects a dry, level spot on which to drop  the
ball, pulls out any long  clumps of grass  or
weeds that may interfere, looks his whole line
and backfield over most carefully and makes
sure they are all properly set.  He  also notes
the set of the opponents and where his greatest
danger is liable to come from; he scans again
the force and direction of the wind, takes his
final look at the bars and uprights, cleans and
dries his hands, takes his own set and—calls for
his ball.  Here again it is useless, in my opinion,
to try to coach on the point by correspondence.
After all, granting native talent, it's  practice
that does it.

It it's a place kick for goal you wish to try the
formation is exactly the same, save that one
of the tandem men on the right must come back,
kneel down on the right hand side and in front
of the kicker and stretch out his hands and
arms toward the snapper, indicating exactly
where he wants to get the ball.  When it comes
back, all he has to do is to adjust it as quickly
as possible, place it down to the ground in the
manner he is accustomed to holding it for any
try-at-goal after touchdown, or as his particular coach or the kicker may desire him to do,
keep cool, hold steady and—the goal is either
made or missed.  If it doesn't go across the
goal line remember the ball isn't dead, or

even sick: it's the livest thing you ever saw. Go
for it, as you would for any punted ball.

If you would like to pull off a forward pass
or try a trick run around the end from a place
kick formation here's one may suit you:

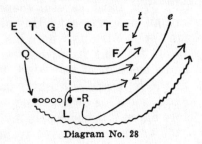

Diagram No. 28

The ball is snapped to R, who places it, as
usual, *on the ground.* L advances and makes
a fake swing at it, but takes care to miss
it; he then goes on as his arrow line indicates.
Meantime Q is dropping back and is in position
to get a quick "float-up" to him of the ball by
R right after L has made his bluff thereat and
gone on out of the way. Q takes the ball for a
run around his own right end, with interference as shown.

Instead of holding it for a run it would be
easy enough for Q to make a forward pass to
any eligible men of his side: these could go in
all manner of directions and to all kinds of
places, as on a regular Punt formation.

## The Quick Kick.

The quick kick from close formation is being tried more than a little these days. Though it may be essayed with intent to make it an "on-side" kick and in the hope that the eligible back will recover it, this is by no means always the case. Undoubtedly it is of much value to a team to be able now and then to get a good, quick, long kick over the head of the opposing safety man and get the benefit of the ensuing roll, and this not only because of the yardage gained in such kick and roll, but because of the moral consternation thereby thrown into the enemy's camp. You put that safety man "up in the air" for the rest of the game—if it is a close one. If he has a habit of sneaking up to the rush line closer than he should, and you succeed in the early stages of putting a good one over on him, it will spell demoralization with him and his playing for the rest of that game nine times out of ten. Thereafter he is apt to play back much further than he should, and in any event he comes up slowly, hesitating-ly and with a lack of confidence that is apt to affect his tackling as well as his handling of punts, and his contagion is apt to spread to his entire team.

It's a simple thing to do. If you have a right-footed kicker you call for the play some-time when you are over to the left side of the field, on either second or third down, with the

ball 25 or 30 yards or more out from your goal.
Your rearmost back, on close formation, is probably back 4 or 5 yards to start with; he quickly
steps back another, or two, the ball comes back
instantly thereafter, he catches it as usual, steps
two steps to the right and puts his foot into it
right where he is. The rest of the backs block
for him in a common-sense manner, two to the
right and one to the left, although it is sometimes unnecessary to have anyone block on the
left, so quickly does the kicker get his ball
away and so far does he step to the right. Of
course it's a surprise play, and you get a lot of
help from that element. With a kicker who
has practiced it a little and who can keep cool
and not mess the kick itself there is practically
no danger of a block: in fact, relatively speaking, far fewer of the quick kicks are blocked
than of those attempted from punt formation.

If one wishes to incorporate the on-side fea-
ture all they have to do is to keep one very fast
back *behind* the kicker until the latter's foot
has actually collided with the ball. This man,
remaining behind the ball till it is kicked, is on-
side, and if he can get to it he is entitled to take
possession of the pig skin without waiting for
one of the opposition to first touch it. At least
it is his if he so gets it out in the field of play.
By special legislation he may not have such a
kicked ball if the kick takes it across the goal
line. Even though the one man that recovered
it was back of the ball at the instant it was

kicked it goes, in this case, as a touchback (Rule VI, Sec. 15, 2nd para. 1921).

## The Running Attack from Punt Formation.

The rearmost man in the backfield, on a punt formation, should be what is known as a "triple-threat" man—he should be able to run the ends well, pass well and punt well, so the defense may not know what kind of a play is coming off merely because punt formation has been taken.

We have seen that even 12 yards is not too great a distance for him to be back of the rush-line if he intends to punt, though fully three yards less than than that would be better for an end run, could he but manage to shorten his distance without the change being observed.

I give below the usual end run from this formation. With an unbalanced formation the assignment of interference is often a little different. In going to the right the snapper should lead the runner by four or five feet, but if the run is around left end it is better to snap it straight at him, as he must delay in his position a bit anyway until his interfering backs can cut across to the left and get in front of him.

A lengthy description of the play with full details would be far from valueless, but lack of space forbids and I can only urge that teams not familiar with the theory of the play pull it off substantially as I have shown.

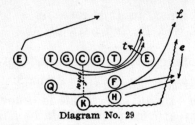

Diagram No. 29

All teams have the close-up backs on punt formation bucking into the line, and some of them have double passes, concealed ball plays, fake end runs that finally unfold as bucks, etc. Particular care should be taken by a coach to have a team equipped with a strong buck through center in case the opposing center drops back off the line and takes out to the side for some reason or other.

A whole game could easily be played by a team using punt formation only, so far as number and variety of plays is concerned, and so it is impossible to give more than a few diagrams of such. Here is a nice trick play that often goes well:

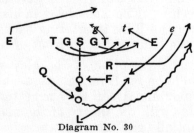

Diagram No. 30

Just before the ball is to go into play F slips to the left (o) and takes up position right back of the ball. Suppose from this position he has a buck thro the line; or else he can act as interferer for either Q or R, either for bucks or for short end runs; and if he will take pains to be back 5 yards he may make forward passes to the ends and tackles, and he can blaze the way on double pass plays between Q and R. Now assume that he has shown his usefulness a few times in some such plays at the position designated; then the stage is set for the special play I have illustrated above. The ball is snapped to F, who draws it back as though to make a forward pass to the left end. As the ball is snapped Q starts around to the right behind F, takes the ball off his backstretched right hand and keeps on going for a sweeping run around his own right end, with R and L and linemen getting into the interference as shown.

With the same maneuver, and F bluffing a pass to the right, R can make an end run of it to the left.

This is known as a "picking the cherry" play: You can find a way to incorporate the basic idea thereof into almost any formation.

Forward passes from punt formation will be discussed under the chapter on that subject.

Trust me, it will pay you to study Punt Formation—and then to *study it again.*

## CHAPTER XII.

### FORWARD PASSING.

When, years ago, the Rules Committee finally decided to permit forward passing, it did so in the hope that such a play might open up the game and so result in a less dangerous sport than had been in vogue up to that time. The author, in suggesting to the Committee such incorporation, had this thought in mind also, but that was not all. I had seen such a play accidentally pulled off in an actual game and realized at once how much more interesting and spectacular the game of football would become if only forward passing were allowed, and I had no doubt that in time such a play would come to be relied upon as a dependable method of advancing the ball. That stage of development has now been reached in the evolution of our great college game.

No longer is the possibility of a forward pass at almost any stage of the game regarded as a mere lurking threat. So many big games have been won and lost of late by the air route that all coaches are alive to the fact that they must include in their system of attack a department of forward passing if they would keep pace with the ongoing procesion. And even teams that resort to its use with the utmost reluctance recognize that they must at least endeavor to frame some defense against such a mode of attack.

A number of writers have given detailed and fairly clear instructions as to how a forward pass may or should be thrown, but I do not think there is need for this here: all school boys, even in the grammar grades, are now fairly familiar with the basic principles involved. It is known to all that the ball must be made to rotate about its long axis in order to throw a spiral. In the case of a passer possessed of a large hand and long fingers it is possible to secure a firm clutch of the ball by grasping it a little from one end. To get a better grip the finger tips are usually distributed over the rough lacing of the ball, and this enables the passer to draw the throwing hand down and under the ball as it is thrown. This hand movement is, of course, what causes the rotation and results in the ball traveling with more speed and under better control toward its objective.

Passers with small hands and short fingers cannot always get a firm grip of the ball in this manner and so must often be content to place the ball more flatly on the throwing hand, somewhat diagonally across the palm. Then, as the ball is released, the hand is drawn smartly inward which again results in giving it a spiralating movement.

This last method is good for a pass of not much more than 30 yards, as a rule, while the former is good for many more yards in the hand of a good passer. This information is of value to a safety man on defense, who can be guided to some extent in deciding how far back to play under certain circumstances, if he knows how opponents' forward passer makes his passes.

Overhand passing is undoubtedly to be preferred to sidearm or underhand. Passes of the latter kind are slower in coming off; they are apt to travel too low and hence are more apt to be broken up or intercepted, and they are never good for as much distance as the overhand passes. One should, in short, throw a football with about the same kind of overhand shoulder snap as is used in throwing a baseball.

A written description of the mechanics of throwing a baseball curve is easily possible, but personal demonstration and practice are far better; and so it it is with learning to throw spirals in forward passing a football.

Underhand passing may be used for short, lateral-pass purposes, while the old end-over-end pass of a football is no longer to be thought of for any purpose; it is completely out-of-date.

Occasionally it is desired that the forward pass shall be executed with all possible rapidity, —to an end or back, for instance, who has not gone much, if any, beyond the line of scrimmage. Here speed is requisite either because it is realized that the intended catcher cannot, in the nature of the play, remain uncovered for longer that a very brief interval, or else the play as designed has left the passer few or no blockers to protect for him while making the pass. This often calls for a basketball pass. On catching the ball with both hands from the snapperback, the passer does not take the time to adjust it carefully in one hand but shoots it out again immediately from the chest *with both hands,* thereby getting rid of it in a minimum of elapsed time after its receipt. Of course, it is good for short distances only.

It makes no difference whether a forward pass is made with the right hand or the left hand. In fact, it is often advantageous to have a left-handed passer in your backfield, as the ball coming off a back's left hand is always more or less of a surprise to the charging defensive players.

To be a success as a forward passer one must be able to do something more than merely throw a good spiral. He should have a quick eye to enable him to find quickly his eligible catchers; he must be able to keep cool and avoid getting unduly excited else he will be hurried into throwing the ball wildly before there is any real need of throwing it at all; he should be able to fend off well with his free arm and to dodge nimbly so he may be able to hold the ball for a considerable period of time if necessary while waiting for his catchers to get into uncovered territory.

## Passes of Different Distance.

In general, it may be said that forward passes are either short, long or of medium length. The short ones are usually employed with intent to compel opponents' secondary defense to get back further and stay back longer. All teams are familiar with the short passes that go to the ends over the middle of the line. In these one end usually goes down about 5 yards and cuts in while the other goes about 10 and then turns in. If the defensive backer-up covers the close-in end the ball is thrown over his head to the end that has gone deeper, while if the backer-up covers the rear end the pass is made to the short man. In this pass the halves go out to the right and left respectively in order to draw the opposing halves out after them and away from the ends. Complimentary plays are executed in exactly the reverse manner, the ends going out while the halves go across the scrimmage line and in.

The varying running and bucking close formations render widely differing kinds of passes possible, according to the peculiarities of the formation. Much depends on what kind of stock formation you use just how your forward passes can best be worked out. I will outline a few from simple formation, the principles of which can be adapted to almost any formation.

Diagram No. 31

Here F is shown making the pass, but if Q is the better passer he can take the snap, run back 5 yards with the ball, wheel and make the pass while F takes over Q's job in going down field for it. This pass is usually pulled off so quickly as to require few or no men remaining back for protection.

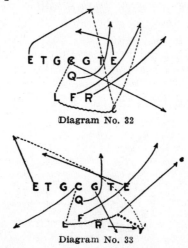

Diagram No. 32

Diagram No. 33

These are other examples of basically sound pass plays. The first is usually a short one, made on the run. Note its resemblance to a bona fide run by the left half around his own right end.

The lower diagram illustrates a pass that may be either short or long as desired. And sometimes the left end is instructed to cut over sharply to the right after crossing the scrimmage line.

Note how the center after snapping the ball, comes out of the line and scampers to the side toward which the pass is to be made, with intent to make it safe by being on hand to tackle a possible interceptor.

For the sake of variety we will now show an unbalanced line with a short, quick pass going to the tackle on the short side. In this case the end playing alongside the tackle will have to drop back a yard in order that the tackle may be considered the end man of the rush line for the time being. To compensate for the loss of the real end from the line a back must slip up

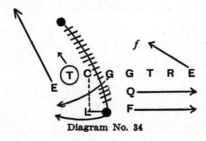

Diagram No. 34

to and go on the line somewhere else. This usually takes place on the other side of the ball.

The pass should be made high so the tackle will have to reach well up into the air for it, and if he is a tall man, so much the better. Note that the left end has gone in the same general direction—and right at the opposing half back, who will usually cover the end, thus leaving the eligible tackle unmolested. The right end gets the attention of the opposing full back. In the unbalanced formation here shown the guard—middle man of the line—comes to the short side for safety and protection both.

## Backs Up His Own Pass.

Nowadays it would be noted in a trice by the defense that an end had dropped back a yard in this manner; but it's not so easy to note a circumstance of this character in time when performed via the "quick shift" route, all other members of the offensive team making a quick shift simultaneously. That is one of the main values of a quick shift; it masks forward passes so well.

Should the defensive half cover the tackle on the above play the passer knows that just beyond that half, in the same direction, is stationed his eligible end, and he makes the pass now to him, over the head of the advancing half.

The tackle should never go more than 5 yards

down and 2 out or he will surely run himself into a secondary defense man who will break up the pass. The passer should not take time to bluff in some other direction but should get it into the hands of the tackle as quickly as possible. If opponents are playing a "box" defense with only six men on the scrimmage line and with the center backing up one tackle and the full back backing up the other tackle, that means they have nobody covering a good-sized circular area right back of the middle of the line. In such case, the tackle should go down and turn *in,* instead of out, and he will have an empty country in which to perform. This play is an excellent variant to the other two described above.

Of late years another kind of short pass is coming very rapidly into favor the country over. It is called the "screen" pass, from the fact that the rush line of the offensive team is instructed not to bother at all to block opponents on the scrimmage line, but to go right thru and clean up the secondary defense, either by actually cutting them down, regardless of whether the ball has as yet come down and been caught by their eligible man, or else by getting in front of the secondary men and presenting their bodies as a real obstruction. Notwithstanding their resistance is only passive, it is mighty hard for a secondary man to get around them or throw them out of the way in time to dispute possession of the ball with the eligible

catchers of the offense. The play is outlined
below:

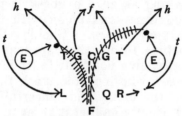

Diagram No. 35

Here it will be noticed that the offensive
backs all remain in their own backyard and protect the passer. This blocking on their part is
necessary because of the fact that the linemen
have not checked up the charging opposition
in the slightest, so the backs needs must stop
them.

This play, it is often urged, is always played
illegally, in that—so it is claimed—the offensive linemen block out the defensive backs before the ball has been caught. No doubt they
sometimes do, but the play is not ipso facto
illegal; it *can* be legally played and, indeed,
generally is. As a matter of fact, if the pass
can be gotten to the hands of the catching
end in a hurry it is nearly always in his possession before the linemen can possibly get to the
secondary defensive men. The point is that the
interference of these linemen is particularly
effective on this pass just because they do not
stop to look and determine by eyesight when

the pass has been caught before they start for their man. They depend on "timing" the thing—making as good a guess as possible of the elapsed time—and along with this guess, they *take a chance*. Should they have the misfortune to cut the opponent down too soon it is probably not their fault but the fault of the passer, who took too much time in getting rid of the ball. They cheerfully pay the occasional penalty and let it go at that.

There is a tendency in the world of football to urge officials to watch such plays very carefully, and of course they should. But their trouble is that of every human being—they cannot have eyes on two rather separated places at the same time, and so it is difficult at times to judge whether the play was legally executed or not.

Delay of some sort by the passer is often necessary where it is difficult to throw the eligible men into uncovered spots.

Here is one—a forward pass preceded by a double pass:

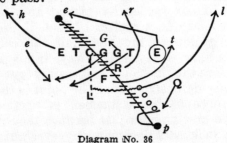

Diagram No. 36

In the above diagram it may be pointed out
that the pass could well be made to R at r, or
to L at l, equally as well as to E at e.

In the following diagram we note the pass is
much longer, and in order that the ends may
have time to get down as far as is desired a
maneuver involving still greater delay in getting rid of the ball is resorted to in the backfield.

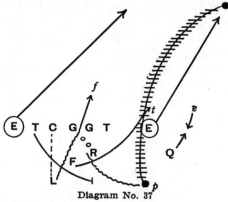

Diagram No. 37

In the above play L, taking the snap, makes
a bluff buck into the line, passes it to R, then
keeps on thru and takes off f. R runs back and
out to the point p and, under the blocking protection of Q, F and the left tackle, who has
dropped back, heaves a long pass between the
two ends, who have raced far down and diagonally out. Some dependence must be placed
on the element of surprise in hoping for a long
enough delay in the direct charge of opponents.

The following is the way a highly successful triple pass, followed by a long forward pass, worked out in a game my Georgia Tech. team played:

The snap was taken by the quarter who took it to the left tackle who ran to the right, passing it to the right half as he went. The latter then passed it to the left half who had been dropping back, and who then (under the protection of the left tackle, the right half and the full back) made a 50-yard pass from the point p to the quarter, who had hustled on down field thru the hole in the line left vacant by his left tackle coming out when he gave the tackle the ball. Note how the two ends drew the two dangerous secondary men out of the way. (Dia. No. 38.)

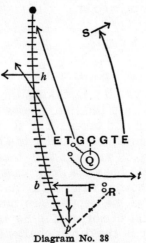

Diagram No. 38

## Passes From Punt Formation.

It is difficult to concoct as many good running and bucking plays from punt formation as can be played from close formation, whereas it is easier to forward pass from punt than from close. The fact that in the case of punt formation opponents take a widely different defensive set accounts in part for this, but more is explained by the fact that the offensive ends go out wider and the backs play further back.

It is perfectly possible to make the "screen" pass from this formation as well as from close formation, and the short, quick pass to the tackle as well as on close formation. I might add that in handling spread or open formations coaches try to figure out ways and means of making not only a tackle eligible to receive a

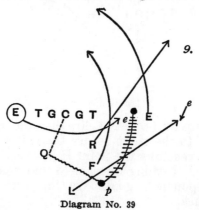

Diagram No. 39

pass but also guards, and even the center himself.

Here is a delayed pass which was first exhibited by the University of West Virginia. Details were somewhat different but I illustrate the principle from an ordinary punt formation. (Diag. No. 39.)

Or the quarter could go out to the right and get a somewhat similar, tho longer pass behind the screen of other eligible catchers from the rear back. A half on the right side could go to the left and take the same pass.

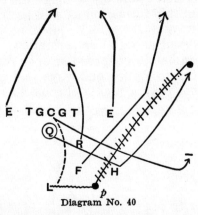

Diagram No. 40

In this play (Dia. No. 40) the quarter would start out to the right before the ball was snapped. On reaching the point H he cries "Hike," just before turning down field and heading toward opponent's goal. On this cry the ball comes back.

Working the play to the left the front half in the tandem would start ahead of the snap and "Hike" the play, while on the diagonally backward run.

Of course, there should also be some running plays with these men in motion ahead of ball. Particular attention is called to the fact that I have outlined practically no forward passes in which the direction of the pass is more sharply toward the boundary line than toward opponents' goal line. I do not think passes should ever be made that are less than at a forward angle of 45 degrees. Passes that go out to the side are often intercepted and then run back all the way for touchdowns by the opposition. They are simply too dangerous. The best thing to do is not to make any such.

This brings me to the point of emphasizing that no forward pass ought ever to be attempted without the coach having figured out who can, and what players *must* back up the pass. It is not enough to provide protection for the passer. If provision has not been made for a possible interception of the pass by opponents it is certainly a faultily constructed play and ought not to be attempted.

Of course the passer, for one, is always expected to back up his own passes and there is no reason why he should not. Usually he is so intent on the job of making an accurate pass and on watching whether it is caught that he forgets his backing-up duties; but I never accept that as an excuse for him not being on the spot when disaster overtakes the play.

Ofttimes one of the other backs can be spared from the play to go out and "make it safe". Generally, however, all the backs are deployed into enemy territory to act as eligible catchers.

As a rule one of the linemen can be brought back and sent out to reinforce a pass. In the case of a balanced line this man is usually the center rush; while, with unbalanced line, the guard nearest to the snapper is the man designated to come out and back it up.

Here is a very long forward pass from the punt formation:

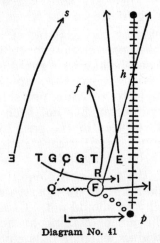

Diagram No. 41

In planning a forward pass coaches usually

rely on one or other of the following ideas
for the success of the play:

1.   Sending a mass of men to a given spot.
Only one of these is expected to try for the ball
while the remainder act as a screen for him.

2.   Sending all the possible eligible catchers
in different directions and different distances
from the passer in the expectation that one of
them at least will discover himself in territory
uncovered by the opposition.  All the eligible
catchers, save the one that is to take the pass,
run close to the secondary defense men in order
that the latter may see and cover them while
letting the one dangerous  man go uncovered.

3.   Making a high pass to a very tall man
who is expected to reach up into the air and get
it before it can come down to where a shorter
man of the rival team can reach to it.

4.   Relying on the blinding speed  of a particular player to carry him past a defensive
man trying to cover him.  In such case the
route of the sprinting catcher  is  carefully
charted for him in advance and the ball is
then thrown well in front of where he is and
in the direction were it is known he will proceed.  Here the eligible catcher simply out-
strips his opponent who, as a mere tag-after,
fails to be in position to dispute possession of
the ball when it comes down.

5.   Opening up the pass play identically as
the same team plays a certain  strong running

or bucking play, so that the defensive team is misled into the supposition that it is the same running or bucking play that has been creating havoc with them; whereupon the secondary men come up rapidly to stop it only to find they have run themselves under a forward pass.

If a passer has time before making the pass he should make a fake always in the direction opposite to the one in which he intends to throw. This fake should be made not only by looking and aiming in the wrong direction, but also by actually striding out with the left foot in that false direction and making a firm stamp of the left foot, followed instantly by a withdrawal thereof and a rethrust of the same in the correct direction. This false footwork will do more toward deceiving the opposition than anything else as to where the pass is going.

## CHAPTER XIII.

## THE HEISMAN SHIFT, OTHER SHIFTS AND SPREAD FORMATIONS.

When a team on the offense lines up with more linemen on one side of the ball than on the other and retains that set formation until the ball is snapped into play, it is said to have an unbalanced line. But when a team, after seemingly assuming a settled position or formation, rapidly shifts one or more of its men to new positions, and then shoots the ball into play immediately after those men have come to a stop in their shifting movement the case is referred to as a "quick shift."

These quick shifts have rapidly been coming into favor the last few years, tho for a long time Minnesota and Georgia Tech. were about the only prominent colleges that seemed to value them highly. Dartmouth also began to use them with much success some years ago, and now many teams make use of the principle in one form or other.

Some teams keep their linemen stationary—either balanced or unbalanced line—and shift the backs, or some of the backs, only. Others draw back from the scrimmage line some or all of the linemen before the shift maneuver is performed and these linemen shift into new positions simultaneously with the shifting of the backs.

Of course, the plan in such quick shifts is to throw against a particular section or point of the defense a preponderance of offensive strength, and do it so quickly that the defense will not have time to assemble its men to that location to stem the heavy onslaught before the ball shall have gone into play. With this in mind it is clear that the men should all be moved simultaneously and with as great speed as possible, and after such preliminary move has been executed and completed that the ball shall be put in play immediately, else the defense will be able to shift reinforcements to the threatened spot in time to nullify the advantage gained by the offense in a preconcerted and well executed shift.

During the last ten and more years defense against such quick shifts has been carefully studied. Much practice in quick shifting on defense has been put in by teams that have had to go up against quick shifting offensives, with result that it has been ascertained that the defense can always shift quite as rapidly as can the offense. There is this difference; that the offense knows what play is coming off after the shift has been completed, while the

defense does not know; and tho the latter may
have brought up a sufficient number of men to
repel the attack, these defensive men do not
have a long enough interval of time in which
to "size up" and correctly diagnose the nature
of the play that is about to be sent at them.
And it is the business and purpose of the offense never to let the defense have any more
time for such diagnosing, after the shift has
been completed, than is absolutely necessary
to conform to the rule requiring them to come
to a full stop.

We will now proceed to a study of some of
these shifts. The following diagram shows
how the players of a team line up prior to the
snapping of the ball, for execution of the Heisman Shift:

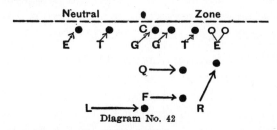

Diagram No. 42

It is obvious that the ball cannot be moved or
changed from the position where it is "down,"
and so all movement, to throw a preponderance
of force to one side or other of the ball, must
be made by the players having possession of
the ball. So, at a given word or sign from the

quarterback or the center, or any other player desired, the men involved in the shift proceed to its speedy execution. In the above diagram it will be noted that the center does not come back from the ball as do all the others. He would only have to go right back to a position over the ball again in order to snap it, and so for him to jump back and jump forward again is but lost motion and wasted effort, besides compelling him to run the risk of losing his balance and making a bad snap.

As the signal is given for the shift, the snapperback quickly bends down over the ball and, simultaneously, all the other players jump to their new stations. In the above diagram I have shown by arrow lines in just what direction each player should jump and how far.

In the following diagrams I have shown just what the formation looks like *before* the shift (top diagram) and what it looks like *after* the shift (bottom diagram). Observe how the preponderance of man power swings from the median line (passing thru the stationary ball) to the *right* side of that same line (middle diagram) or to the left side (lower diagram), according to whether the shift was to the right or to the left:

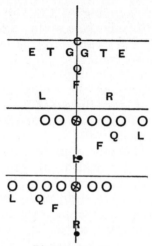

Diagram No. 43

After the shift has been completed we have a not unusual unbalanced Right Formation (middle diagram) or Left Formation (lower diagram) from which the usual plays, end run, off-tackle smash, center buck, forward pass and what not, are developed the same as tho no quick shift had preceded the formation.

This shift may be performed either by a jump or by a cross step (The Glide). In both, the players set squarely on both feet. In executing the jump they simply jump off both feet, go as far as they can ordinarily and come down on both feet. The instant all those feet land back on terra firma, which should be simultaneously, the ball is shot back by the snapperback, which snapping of the ball permits the players to galvanize into action again instantly afterwards. They can either be informed that the ball has so gone into play by the quarter calling "Hike!" simultaneously with the landing of the feet and the snapping of the ball, or they can all learn the exact instant by having their minds educated or attuned to the rhythm of the movement.

The Glide is almost equally simple. If going, say, to the right a back would cross his left leg over his right, then draw his right leg from behind and out to the right and place that right foot just where he would want it, in relationship to the left foot, so that he would have the sprinter's set for starting. Next, he would twist his body backward to left, so as again to face the line of scrimmage,—all of which, goes on a smooth steady count of "One, two, three," and on the fourth count he would "CHARGE!"

The Glide is a bit slower than the Jump, but it is easier to come to a complete halt by its use than by employing the Jump. Also, it is easier to keep one's poise and get a better "set" for charging than from the jump.

Of course, it is perfectly legal to hop, skip, jump or do anything else as a method of locomotion in thus shifting from one spot to another; but I have described in detail the two ways that translate a player with the greatest ease, smoothness and speed.

## Other Advantages of Quick Shifts

Besides assembling a considerable force of men at a given spot in a short space of time, a quick shift of this character is good for certain other things not usually taken advantage of. One of the most important is that by its use a coach is enabled to have his backs shift in different directions and differing distances from each other, and from the way the linemen shift, on different plays. In other words he can thus throw his men into a great variety of differing formations while the ball, coming back so soon after the strange formation has been assumed, allows opponents no time in which to "size-up" that it is different from the others; or, if some of the defensive players should be quick enough to note the change, they have not time to notify their comrades thereof nor to confer with each other as to the best way to meet it.

Again, the mere general kaleidoscopic movement of so many men tends to confuse the defensive player, to say nothing of the fact that if the offensive linemen are tall, the defensive linemen have difficulty peering thru and between them and keeping the offensive backs plainly in sight.

Another detail of vantage in a quick shift of this character is that the shifting offensive players are moving out in the general direction which they will usually take after the ball is snapped. The defensive team, to meet this, must move out in the safe direction; but that direction is for them the opposite of the way they ought to be going, for of course, the defensive team usually charges *in* not *out* as the ball goes into play, and so they are liable to be caught on the move in the very direction the attack would have them go.

It may as well be admitted, however, that it is difficult for linemen to make such a quick shift and land in a posture that is good for a quick, hard charge immediately to follow; and for this reason many coaches have their linemen take what stations they desire on the line of scrimmage and be done with it. These execute no shift whatever, but are all set and ready for a fierce, hard charge the instant the backs have completed their shift.

Some coaches leave the ends and tackles on the line and have only the guards drawn back of the scrimmage line. These guards then jump, like Siamese twins, either to right or left of snapper and by so doing lengthen either the right side or the left side of the line. Of course, the tackle and end on the short side of the ball close in on their center and so tighten up the line while the backs are shifting behind the scrimmage line

The Dartmouth shift is very similar to that employed by Georgia Tech., but in the Minnesota shift not only do the backs and linemen shift to one side or the other in this general way, but the end from the short side rapidly comes back into the backfield. This leaves only six men on the rush line. But while the end is coming back the halfback farthest away from him is, simultaneously, slipping up onto the strong side of the rush line to make the seventh required man.

Tho, as a rule, coaches using quick shifts spring their plays from an unbalanced line, which means that the guards have both shifted to the same side of the center, it is a good plan to have them "split normal" now and then. Thus, the right guard would jump to his usual position at the right side of the snapper, and the left guard steps back up into his usual position at the center's left, while the backs shift right or left without reference to what the guards do. This would seem silly but, strange to say, the defensive line is often puzzled by such a maneuver. Each defensive guard is ready to swear, after having watched such a split, that *both* offensive guards came to his side of the center, and so each shifts out wide to meet them. As a consequence there is often found an enormous hole straight thru center, under such circumstances.

Of course, the fact that the play itself is preceded by a quick shift does not affect or alter the principles of interference by the offensive players in the slightest. The assignment of duties to the interferers is detailed and accurate, and the interferers have their job to do as usual in taking off tacklers and cleaning up the secondary defense just as tho the start had been from standing formation.

Sometimes it is found that one player cannot jump as far as the rest altho it is, perhaps, requisite he should do so. In that case he must be labored with till he can jump that far, or the rest must be geared down to his distance, or else he must be set aside in favor of a man that can shift further. This is usually the trouble where a tall guard is paired with a short one; the latter has not sufficient leg length to enable him to shift as far as the long-legged guard.

There is a quick running shift used by Coach Glenn Warner, sometimes, that is very pretty in execution and that must be prepared for else it works havoc against a green defensive team. Its principle is as follows:

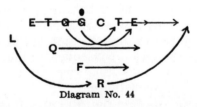

Diagram No. 44

The arrow lines indicate how and to where the players run at the given command to shift. The diagram below shows that the formation has been exactly reversed after the shift has been completed.

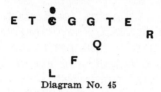

Diagram No. 45

A running shift of this character may also be used to advantage in springing to positions for a wide open or "spread" formation, especially if the spread shows more men on one side of the ball than on the other  Thus, suppose we line our team up as in the following diagram:

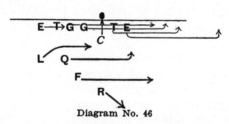

Diagram No. 46

From this we throw them with extreme rapidity into the following one-sided open formation, with the strength to the right.

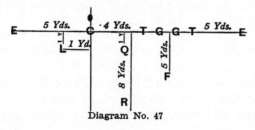

Diagram No. 47

Before the offensive team started to make this big quick shift, the defensive team had no way of knowing whether the ball was going to be snapped with the offensive team all set to charge hard right from the positions they were occupying in the first diagram, or whether that offensive team was suddenly going to start running pell-mell to the opposite side of the center and the ball. In the first case the defensive players should be set low and have their muscles tensed for a fierce charge forward into the opposing line where it stands; but if the second case is to come off, then they must be on their toes and alert to start out running to their own *left* in order to be over on the other side of the ball as soon as the offensive players, and this means they must be ready to rise up and spring for dear life, sizing up the coming new formation as they go. This uncertainty puts a terrific strain on the defense compelled to meet such a line of varied attack. A well-drilled team of good players can play "Hob" by using such an attack. I will diagram a few plays from this open formation, as many coaches of light teams are sadly in need of some such formation. In each case I will assume that the running shift above described has been completed and all is ready for the snapping of the ball. Though showing the formation spread to the right only, it is obvious the same set and plays can be worked to the left side of the ball with equal facility.

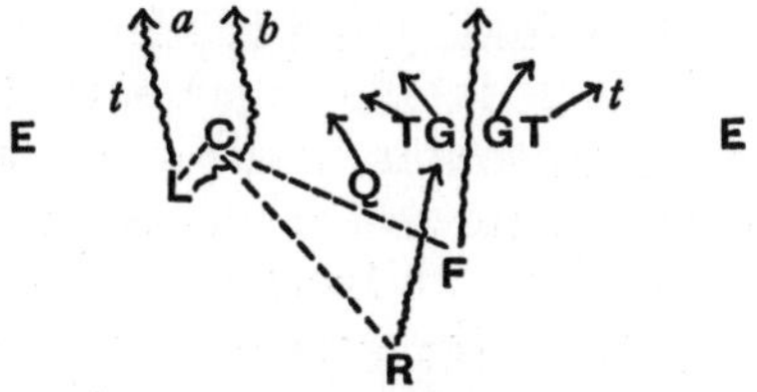

Diagram No. 48

In the first place opponents must *always* set one man (usually a tackle—and so one big man of the opposition is held down to position by one small man on the offense) opposite L. If at any stage of the game L notes there is no one opposite him he instantly calls for the ball from C, no matter what signal may already have been given. The latter instantly floats the ball out to him and down the field he goes, simply because there is no one in front of him. Or, if there is nobody in the gap between C and T, he calls for the ball again and makes his gain thru this gap, while C is turning the opposing tackle to the left. These two possibilities are shown by L's wiggling lines—a and b.

Next we have a direct snap to F. This may be made between the legs of the snapper, as in the ordinary snap, or else tossed out to the side in front of the right leg, tho it will take practice to get speed on the ball and accuracy in getting it in *front* of F, and neither too high nor too low. This is a plain buck by F straight at the four big linemen in front of him. Experience with the formation is all that is needed to tell

a coach or team that Q and the left tackle must
be cautioned to look for opponents playing in
the gap next to center, while the right tackle
and end will have to watch out for others playing in the gap between them.

By lining up a bit closer to the line—say,
only 6 yards back—it works out well to snap
the ball to the rear back, R, for a plunge thru
the same place, with F leading as a free interferer.

Again, the ball can be snapped to F, who
will draw it back as tho to make a pass to the
left end. As he does so R comes tearing down
to his right and plucks it off his right hand,
while Q is blocking out to the right the opposing tackle, who is charging through the outside
gap.

Below I diagram an end run from the same
formation:

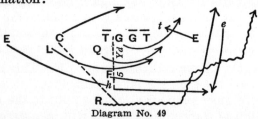

Diagram No. 49

In this the left end has started with the rest
on their rapid shift to the right; but, whereas the
others all come to a stop when they reach their
proper stations he keeps on running and
"hikes" the play at the point h, then continues

on and, with F, takes the opposing end. The snap should "lead" R as far as possible. Pulled off with speed and confidence, and getting interference into it, the play goes with startling success.

It should be easy for any fairly experienced coach or player to work out no end of good forward passes from this formation. Both F and R are in splendid position to make them, and both ends are in strategical positions to receive them, either short or long passes. L and Q are in equally advantageous locations to receive forward passes, and the formation is so widespread that it will compel the opposition to spread equally wide on the defense to meet it. This means they will not be close enough together to support one another against a varied attack.

By having Q line up *on* the scrimmage line as he runs over to his position from preceding "left formation," while the left end is taking station 1 yard back, the center himself is made eligible to receive a forward pass, and is found nearly always free to do so about 15 yards down field and slightly toward the short side.

Again, by having Q on the line the right end may be back a yard and the right tackle will be eligible for the pass. Also, the screen pass can be made with ease to either the end or the center by either F or R. Just to show the unique variation in forward passing that is possible from such a formation, I will outline another

forward pass that could not easily be described
without a diagram:

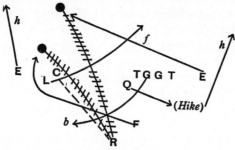

Diagram No. 50

The defense is misled into watching Q (who
started to the right in advance of the snap and
"hikes" the ball on the run, as shown), and L,
(who is perfectly eligible and who gets the attention of the opposing full back). The left
end draws his half back out and away from
where the pass is going, and meantime, the right
end and F are both making for uncovered territory to the left. Even if one of them is "spotted" the other is almost sure to be free. The
left guard has come out to the left to protect the
passer, R, and then backs up the pass itself,
along with R.

To finish, I cannot resist pointing out that
this is an excellent kicking formation as well,
for all the linemen have to do is to halt a bit
sooner in their running shift, leaving a gap of
but a yard or two between them and center, and

then the other three backs give plenty of protection to the punter, R, who puts the ball straight down the field in front of the four big linemen, all of whom can leave at once and be down like ends on the opposing safety man by the time the ball gets there.

## CHAPTER XIV

## TEAM DEFENSE IN FOOTBALL.

Formerly there were as many ways of setting and playing a football team on defense as on offense. Nowadays, however, it is pretty well recognized that there are three different defensive sets that are considerably superior to any and all others. These three vary but little, so far as an inspection of diagrams will disclose. For purposes of easy comparison, I give them all together.

### A—Center in the Line.

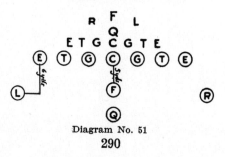

Diagram No. 51

## B—Loose Center (Center Playing back of the line.)

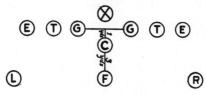

Diagram No. 52

## C—Box Defense.

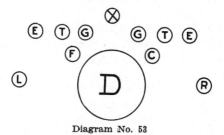

Diagram No. 53

The advantage of keeping the center in the line on defense is that thereby seven men are spread out over the length of the scrimmage line, which means that the gaps between these seven men are smaller than if the center played behind the line, leaving only six men to safeguard a scrimmage line of the same length. This adds thickness or density to the line and makes it more impervious to bucking assaults.

Of course a center playing in the line could not be expected to get out of the line and tackle at the ends, and so the brunt of the tackling would fall upon the shoulders of the fullback stationed right behind the center of gravity of the attack. If the fullback is a large, strong, rugged player with worlds of endurance this works out all right, although many coaches will not burden the fullback so heavily on defense, preferring to save him as much as possible so he will always keep strong enough to deliver dependably on offense.

Now glance for a moment at diagram B, in which the center is shown as playing back of the scrimmage line a yard or two. In this position the "roving" center shifts as his judgment dictates, always setting himself opposite where he diagnoses the attack will come or, in the case of a shifted line by the offense, stationing himself opposite the center of gravity of the attack. This means that he will get the brunt of the tackling, for he will be the first man in the secondary defense to go in and meet the play.

In this defense the fullback is entrusted with the job of backing up the loose center as he stands three or four yards back of that center, as a rule, where the formation is balanced. If it is an unbalanced formation he still plays back a total five yards, but keeps more of an eye to the short side of the line and looks out for forward passes. He shuttles right or left as the attack unfolds, always keeping his relative position with reference to his center; if he is on the left of his center when the play starts he should be found tackling on the left and the center on the right when the runner comes through, and vice versa, if he was on the right hand of the runner when the play started. It follows that in so shuttling right and left *as a pair* it will be well if the loose center very slightly overruns the runner while the fullback slightly underruns him; then they will not be blocking each other off from the runner, and when the latter comes through they will compel him to go between them, and so they will both be able to get at him.

Many teams play formation B until the opposing team forces them back to their own 15 or 20 yard line, when they send the center up into the line (formation A) to help stop the successful bucking. This is rendered feasible because the defensive quarterback is now driven up closer behind his team (else he would be standing behind his own goal line). This means that, to a large extent, he can take over the work and place of the fullback, while the latter is thereby enabled to take over a large part of what had been the center's work. Besides, the quarter dares to come closer because he knows that opponents can hardly kick the ball without sending it over for touchback, nor can they make a very long forward pass without great danger of throwing it clear beyond the end zone; so there is no need of his playing back so far at this juncture.

Formation C is often taken by teams on defense when they have weak or slow tackles, or when they have special reason to fear the enemy's assaults against their tackles. Especially is it good to stop direct bucks straight ahead by halfbacks in quick opening plays, and of course it is better for stopping end runs than either A or B; but this formation leaves a great weakness against forward passes that may be tossed into the large area immediately back of the center and full back, for there is no other player of the defensive side in position to get into this exposed area more quickly than can the opposing ends, who may be shot into it to take such passes. In formation B the fullback would be standing all the time within the circle D, but in formation C neither the fullback nor the center are even near its circumference.

When the opponents take punt formation a considerable change in the set of the defensive team is always necessitated. In the first place both ends and both tackles must play out wider than they do against close formations, else they will be outflanked by a running attack around the end, with the man standing back in kicker's place carrying the ball.

In the second place few teams are willing to entrust the handling of the expected punt to the quarterback alone; so they bring another player back at least part way to help out in this department. This is usually one of the halves. But if a half comes back from one side or other his place must be taken by the fullback, else

the enemy will simply hurl a forward pass to
their end on that side and there will be nobody
there to prevent him getting it.

But if the full leaves the central section to go
to one side then the center must drop back a
little further than usual, else a pass right over
the middle of the line will go over his head, and
there can be no one else to stop it save the center.   These readjustments compel a set something like the following:

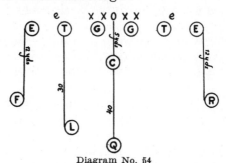

Diagram No. 54

It will be observed that the side backs on defense are back further than they would be
against close formation.   This is because a
passer standing in the kicker's position, 10
yards back, on kick formation, cannot be hurried by the defensive team as much as on close
formation, and so he can make much longer
passes, as a rule, than on close formation. This
means the defensive side backs will do well to
take these probable long passes into their cal-
culations and set further back to start with. Be-

sides they can help better in interference for their punt catcher from a position further back.

The rush line men of a football team on defense are the artillery that batter down the walls of the beleaguered city, while the secondary defense men are the infantry that rush in with their cold steel after the breach has been made. It is the business of the defensive line to "Charge hard with the ball," crowd back the other rush line into the faces of the advancing backs, smash up the interference and thereby force the runner out into the open. The secondary defense men coming up rapidly—as soon as they have made sure that it is a rushing attack and not a forward pass—are now close at hand to dispatch the runner with a deadly tackle.

Linemen must watch and handle *interference*. They must shift and go where the opposing linemen shift and go, and they are compelled to regard the threat of even fake interference. But not so the secondary defense men; they should watch the *ball* all the time and go where goes the man carrying the ball. They follow him like hawks, and when he attempts to come through they must be directly opposite to his place of cut-in and stand ready to make the tackle.

When it comes to stopping forward passes the assignment of work differs but little. The linemen still charge and crowd and smash and fight their way through the offensive line in order to get at the man making the pass. Their endeavor is to crowd him, to compel him to hurl the ball before his eligible catchers shall have had time to reach the locations they deem most favorable for them in which to get the pass. Particularly do the defensive ends try hard to rush the passer.

While the linemen are doing this the backs are covering the eligible catchers coming down, and when the ball itself comes over they must be close to these catchers so they can jump and dispute possession of the ball with them.

On defense linemen should always charge and break through on the *outside* of their man. Guards usually charge straight ahead, but tackles are instructed to charge diagonally in toward the opposing quarter, to "telescope" the opposing line, forcing it more compactly together and so making it more difficult for the offensive backs to prize it apart.

Secondary defense men are in constant doubt whether to go in for an early tackle or to hang back a bit waiting for a possible forward pass to come sailing over the rush line. They should study the opposing backs and note whether *All* the backs are coming forward toward the scrimmage line or whether one of them is running somewhat backward. If the latter, or if he was five yards back to start with and is remaining that far back that means a pass.

Against a punt formation there exists considerable difference of opinion as to whether the defensive ends should hamper the offensive ends from going down field when the offensive team punts, or whether they should pay no attention to the ends going down but shoot in fast and hard for the purpose of blocking the expected kick, or else be on hand to tackle in case it turns out to be a run around end. In the latter case the ends going down under punts would meet with opposition only from the defensive halfbacks.

Probably the best rule to follow is to endeavor to form some idea as to whether it is really going to be a kick. If it is fourth down with lots to go and the ball is in enemy territory, no doubt it will be a kick. Then it might be well for the defensive end to block the other end, unless the ball is being kicked from inside the kicker's own 25-yard line, in which case it would be better for the defensive end to do all he could to block the kick, for if he succeeds in so doing at that place in the field it is likely to result in a touchdown for his team.

## Defense Against Forward Passes.

When it comes to meeting and stopping forward passes linemen have not, as a rule, so much more to learn on top of what they have already learned with reference to ways and means of stopping runs and bucks as might be supposed. In either case their first and supreme duty is to charge. If they have diagnosed the play in advance as a forward pass then their

charge has more intelligence and more directness, and they discard at once all thought of
"going under." Instead they either cover an
eligible man or they rush the passer.

The defensive tackles are usually the only
linemen who are in position to do the first. Playing opposite, or just outside, the offensive ends,
as they often do, they are frequently able to
make a surprisingly big contribution toward
helping out their backs in the matter of taking
care of eligible ends. They charge into those
wingmen with tremendous fury, under pretense
of making a vicious attempt to drive them back
into the backfield interference—as though they
expected a fierce line plunge aimed directly at
them. This usually delays or holds back the
ends until the opposing passer has been compelled to hurl the ball.

Again, when opponents take punt formation
the defensive center often "smells" a forward
pass. At such times he backs out of the rush
line and, standing back three or more yards,
tries to figure which of the eligible offensive
backs he would do well to stay with.

Defensive tackles have been known to correctly size up a forthcoming short pass just over
the rush line to, say, one of the offensive ends.
In such case they might, as usual, charge and
hurry the pass; but if these tactics have been
found unavailing they sometimes take it into
their heads to back up a few steps and hinder
the opposing end from getting undisputed pos-

session of the pass. They must take care, however, lest the opposing general note this tendency and, faking a forward pass, he dive with the ball through the opening created by the defensive tackle's withdrawal.

Outside these instances linemen are seldom urged to try to cover eligible catchers, though spread and freak formations may call on a man to do most anything, no matter how unusual. Ordinarily the best thing a lineman can do to help ruin forward passes is to hurry the passer.

On the secondary defense falls the lion's share of the work of actually wrecking the passes, and here the half backs have an even harder task than the defensive full. The halves must watch the opposing ends all the time. If the latter are plainly trying to box the tackle or help in opening a rush line hole it's a fair sign that it's a buck, not a pass. But if the end is trying to work into a position of clearance from the defensive line then he must at once be suspected of harboring sinister designs.

Secondary defensive men also study all the offensive backs. If all of them have advanced closer to the line than 5 yards it's pretty safe to plunge in; but if one of them is still back that far, and especially if he still has the ball, you can do nothing less than decide instantly that a pass must be coming. Accordingly stay back—and *back up farther still*.

In the case of passes made from the more usual close formations the half (or side-back, as

I prefer to designate the defensive position) sticks with the end rush opposite to him. He *never* lets that end get behind him: he always keeps the end in front of him. If he will always do this any pass made to that end will have to be in front of the side back. This means he will have the advantage of the end in that he will be facing the ball while the end will often have his back toward the approaching ball. In general, play the ball itself in the case of a short pass.

The side back may be shorter than the end, in which case he will not be able to get his hands on the ball as high up as the end. The thing to do here is for the side back, as they jump, to strike the wrist or forearm of the end and knock the end's hand away from the ball. The end will not be prepared to catch the ball with one hand and in all probability he will fail to hold it with the one hand.

Another thing for a defensive player to do when trying to prevent an opponent from getting the pass is to swing the body or hips toward that opponent, even as you go up for the ball. This will put you between him and the ball.

A discussion that takes lots of time each fall in nearly every camp is whether, from the team standpoint, it is better to play territory or eligible men in trying to break up forward passes. That is a question that cannot be answered in a hard and fast manner. Against certain teams

and formations and kinds of passes it will, no
doubt, be better to defend territorially, assigning to each man certain zones to cover; while in
other cases it is just as clear it will be better if
the opposing eligible men are covered as players, each of them being definitely assigned to
one of the defense to be watched and covered.

Against ordinary close-formation passes it is
more usual to play a zone defense; whereas,
when it comes to punt and open formations, it
is oftener the case that coaches instruct their
secondary men how to take and stay with the
eligible receivers. In the case of very long
passes the safety man, and to a lesser extent,
the defensive full always play the man if possible. In any case as soon as the ball has left
the passer's hand every defensive man should
play the ball itself.

Although the side back usually studies the offensive end it is better that he should drop the
end in case an offensive back goes out far to one
side. In such case the side back is the man to
go out with that detached back. The defensive
end must remain in close just as long as possible
in order to smash interference, in case it is a
run, and in order to hurry the passer even when
it is a pass. But if the side back goes out to
guard a detached back that means that someone
else of the defense must take the offensive
end on that side. If the tackle can hold the end
in well and good. If he cannot the full back
will have to look after him. This, it may be

argued, will leave no one back of the middle of the line. True, but this is the kind of time when the defensive center should drop back out of the line. In other words, the mere fact that one man of the offense has gone far out to one side in advance of the snap makes the formation a forward pass threat, and in such case it's always time for the defensive center to think of retreating and getting into his own backyard for the purpose of helping the secondary men break up the expected pass.

It is customary to have the side back playing against the short side of an unbalanced offensive formation, play a little deeper than the one posted against the strong side of the formation.

If an offensive end drops back a yard just before the ball is to be snapped, the defensive end or tackle on that side should at once notify his secondary defense men of the fact in order that they may have an eye on the man that is now the end man on that side of the rush line, usually a tackle.

Defense in these days must at all times take into consideration what the field situation is, what the down, and how great the distance to be gained. Deep in its own territory no team is apt to play forward passes on any down whatsoever; but once beyond their own 35 or 40 yard line it's time for you to begin to worry about them just a little, though not on first down. Near your own goal, if you have held them well, you must count it as strongly probable that they will attempt a pass over your goal line on the fourth down or sooner. When you anticipate a pass the secondary defensive men drop back a yard or two farther, and they should be slower about coming up till they can determine to a certainty just where the ball is, or is going to be. Also this is the time for the center to back out of his line, for the tackles to study whether they can charge the opposing ends back and so prevent them from going down field, for the guards to play a bit higher and study what they can do to help rush the passer, for the ends to set themselves where they can rush the passer with all possible dispatch, and for the safety man to come up to within about 25 yards of the scrimmage line and keep his eyes wide open for the first man coming down for what looks as though it may be a long pass.

Probably the most valuable information a "scout" can bring back with him in these days, after watching a prospective opponent play a game, is accurate information as to how they execute their forward passes. These may be so varied and unique in their method of performance that general instructions do not begin to suffice as a defense against what may come via the air route. Each rival team's passes should be studied carefully by themselves and a special defense devised if possible for each of them.

## Relation of Offense to Defense.

A powerful offense makes a good defense. It not only helps to accustom the players to the mad rush and the wild smash called for to perfect a fierce and unyielding defense, but it also aids wonderfully in the physical conditioning of the players. In addition it crystallizes a team's knowledge of its formations, plays and signals.

## A Few Defensive Hints.

Never wait for the opposing team or the runner to come to you. Always go to him without delay; otherwise you will find it harder to stop him after he has his full steam up. Besides he is eating up ground in your territory, ground you cannot afford to give up to him. Take the battle to him without waiting and stop him before he has penetrated too far into your domain.

Never take it for granted that because you see one of your teammates tackling a runner that you will have nothing to do on that play and that there is no need of your continuing to run on into the play. There is always a very good chance that your comrade will miss his tackle and won't stop the runner, and then you will wish you had kept on running.

Never be content anyway to see just one teammate get hold of the runner. There is no reason why two, three or more men cannot get and have hold of the runner simultaneously every time he is downed. Make yourself personally responsible for the stopping of every play started by opponents.

Follow the ball all the time. If you are near the ball at all times you will nearly always be playing good football. If on offense you will be in position to interfere for the runner if you are close at hand. If you are always near it on defense you will be the man making most of the tackles. If a fumble occurs you will be the man nearest it to always fall on it or pick it up and run for touchdown. If it is a forward pass you will be the one who gets it or breaks it up.

It's a good idea to keep up a running chatter of cheery and encouraging talk to your teammates; keep the life and animation in it all the time. It will not only pluck up their spirits and keep the fight in them but it will help keep your own nerves steady and your jaws set tight.

Never turn your back on the play or shut your eyes in a scrimmage. You must always know just where the ball is, and you cannot know that unless you keep facing the play.

Never give in or admit even to yourself that you are defeated. No matter how tired you are you must always say that the other team is even more tired.

## CHAPTER XV.

## STRATEGY AND SIGNALLING.

Before the game the coach should always take his captain and his signaller out on the field and give it a thorough going over. If it is level and firm everywhere, and there are no natural or artificial mounds, hollows, structures, fences or trees near the boundaries, there remains nothing particular for them to note save the position the sun occupies in the sky and the direction and strength of the wind.

If you win the toss, choose the goal with the sun at your back. Likewise, it is much to your advantage to have the wind behind you rather than blowing toward you. True, you will have to exchange goals at the end of the first quarter, but by that time the sun will not be quite so bright, and perhaps the wind will have died down as the afternoon wears on.

With no especial advantage to either side because of sun or wind, and other things fairly equal, you would prefer to kick off. In the first place a team is nervous and liable to fumble if it has the ball at the outset of the game; better let the other team chance the fumbles deep in

313

its territory by kicking to them. Then, too, you can throw much nearer 100 per cent of your defensive effectiveness into action in the very first two minutes of a game than you can possibly get into your offense at that early stage.

If you have a good stiff wind, do a lot of punting. Make use of that wind while you can. By punting high the ball will be carried far down the field. Then, if you have a reliable defense, you compel opponents to kick against the wind. Barring flukes and fumbles you should, under these circumstances, gain on every exchange of punts.

The best thing generally is to punt from behind your 30-yard line and keep the ball far down in the enemy's territory, especially if you have the wind with you. It matters little that the opposition has the ball. If you have any kind of a defense the opposition will never be able to carry the ball the whole length of the field without having to surrender it for one reason or another. And then, with that fine wind at your back, you promptly pump it all the way back, making them start all over again. As prolonged offensive play is more wearing than defensive the enemy's vitality will be sapped faster than yours. Also the psychological effect is great; it's most disheartening to a team to see its difficult running and bucking gains completely nullified by a powerful swing of one right foot.

And on top of this we have to note that the

STRATEGY AND SIGNALING      315

other team, not daring to enter a punting duel with such a wind against them, and having no choice but to run or buck, thereby reveals the nature of its plays in midfield or in its own territory, not near your goal. Were they to secure possession of the ball deep in your territory without as yet having shown you how their rushing plays unfold, your position would be precarious.

But that is exactly what **you** are trying to do to **them**. You are making them show their hand at a time when it spells no danger to you. Sooner or later they may fumble, or make a bad snap, or you will block one of their punts, or the officials will penalize them (offense usually incurs more penalties than defense), and so get the ball still closer to their goal line. Or perhaps they will punt out of bounds for no appreciable gain, or they will make the mistake of another try at the line on last down when they really ought to punt, and then you will take it away from them on downs.

Some way, you figure, you will ultimately get the ball within the shadow of their goal posts. Then, with your carefully husbanded strength, you will spring your best plays—which they have not yet seen and have not yet learned how to stop and—Blam! you have scored before the enemy has at all realized how it could possibly happen.

Of course, a kicking game of this character will never run up a big score against opponents.

But no strategy of any kind is ever needed against a team that one can defeat by a goodly score. And against opponents considered fully your equal in playing strength you may well be content to win the game even by the narrowest margin. A good punting game and a stiff defense is the system that will come nearest to assuring you victory.

If a team believes it is strong offensively and, at the outset of the game after receiving the kick-off, it finds no great difficulty in rushing the ball for gains, it is a great temptation still to retain possession in the conviction that it can score. That can be done against a weak team —and you may continue to hold the ball. But against a strong team you may not hope to ram it the whole length of the field for a touchdown. In attempting to do so you are but rapidly expending your strength while they are learning how to diagnose and master your plays. As you approach their goal their defense will tighten up and they will take the ball away from you on downs.

A successful end run invariably goes for a longer gain than a buck, but it is very much more likely to be thrown for an absolute loss than is a smash at the line.

A buck is much surer of some gain than is an end run, but the greater gain may be expected from a successful end run.

From the above it follows that if you need a

long gain on the next play you must decide on the end run; while if you need but a short gain a buck is the proper thing.

This is as between these two only. Of course, one may prefer to pass or punt, or to essay a trick play; but the above notes the fundamental difference between the end run and the buck.

On the first down, ten yards to go, the field general must take note of whether the ball is near his goal or near opponents' or near neither. He must take into account the position of the sun, the wind and footing conditions. He also must know what the physical condition of his men is—and that of the opponents. He must reflect on what experience has taught him as to which plays are working well and which are **meeting** with disaster; he must bear in mind whether the ball is wet or dry and the possibility of fumbling. Again, he must bear in mind how far or near it is to the close of the half or to the end of the game.

All these things have their influence in deciding which play to attempt.

Now, in the first place, a bucking game cannot be relied upon to yield an average of 2½ yards. And so to start the first down play with a buck is to attempt a plan in which the odds are against you at the outset. If you were to make say, three bucks in succession and they yielded a total of but 5 yards, and that is quite likely to be the limit, then you would have still 5 yards to go and but one down in which to make it.

But you should know, **and opponents would know,** that you could not expect to make it by another buck. Only a successful end run (discarding for the moment consideration of punts, passes and tricks) can possibly pull things out of the fire. But as the opposing team also knows this it sets itself to stop the expected end run and does so, and you have lost the ball.

But when the referee first called "First Down, ten to go," the opposing team had no idea as to whether you were going to attempt an end run or a buck, and so it could not set itself for any special play. If you try an end run then and it succeeds, it is likely to go 10 yards or more and there you have your first down. Or at least it is likely to go five yards, and then there remain but five yards, with three trials left in which to make it.

If the signaller is safely away from dangerous proximity to his own goal line and he is not yet ready to punt, he is naturally intent on the matter of how best to work the ball far down the field. A good many inexperienced signallers get in a big hurry about this and promptly start playing all their supposedly fine "long gainers" the very first thing. They should not do this.

At the present moment the signaller is not concerned with the problem of a touchdown in the next two minutes. It is only the matter of gaining 10 yards in the next four trials—or less—that need worry him. He should reason that if he can only negotiate the next 10-yard line, and then the next, the touchdown problem will take care of itself.

Now, suppose you receive the kick-off and your catcher is downed with the ball close to your own goal line. If the ball is inside your own 15-yard line most good signallers would order a punt on the very first down. In such a position an end run, double-pass or a trick should never be attempted. You should not attempt an end run until you have the ball fully 25 yards out from your goal.

"Well, how about a buck?"

Yes, undoubtedly a buck is much safer than an end run or trick—unless the trick is one which is not likely to result in a fumble or loss.

A forward pass should never be attempted inside your own 30-yard line; should it be intercepted you will, in all probability, lose a perfectly good game of football right then and there.

So, if you just must try a rushing play or two, let it be a buck. By some lucky chance it might go for a good gain. In that case you still retain the ball and you have it further out— you now have a wider latitude. But if this buck gains nothing you **must** punt the thing out of danger. You ask, ''Why not buck once more, or even twice and then, if we must, punt on the last down?''

The answer is—because you are attempting fate itself by fooling around with that ball for so long so close to your goal line. Your snapper might make a bad snap and sail it back across your own goal line. Or a back might fumble, or one of your men might misunderstand the signal and come running around in the wrong direction, thus unexpectedly colliding with those going in the opposite direction. Those things do happen and they're bad no matter when they happen, but they're much worse if they occur right down by your goal line.

And so, with the ball 15 yards or less from your goal line, you don't make a very big mistake if you order a punt on first down. But if you do elect to hold the ball and rush it, try nothing but the simplest kind of a line buck, preferably through tackle. If you make a gain of less than three yards on that buck, punt on the second down. But if you gained more than five yards you *might* buck again. After that—unless your second buck gave you first down—*punt*—don't buck or do anything else.

After getting the ball worked out, say, 20 yards or more, you can take a little more risk, and the further down the field you get it the greater risk you are justified in taking on the last down to hold it.

Every team is supposed to have several plays of scoring power when used within good striking distance of opponents' goal. But it should not reveal them until they get close to the goal.

If bucks have been going fairly well up to that time, it is customary for the signaller to try to buck it over the short remaining distance. Naturally, he hates to run the risk of being thrown back for a possible loss by attempting an end run. However, his opponents usually are expecting him to reason in that way, and so their line shortens up and the backs come up closer to the linemen. With such defensive changes as these it becomes an all but impossible undertaking to ram it over. Still, we often see teams trying four bucks in succession at such a time when the slightest inspection of the defensive set of the other team should convince anyone of the futility of trying a buck.

But if the signaller will look, and if he sees them so set, then it's a perfectly safe proposition to call for an end run, and he will find the play sweeping around with almost ridiculous ease.

Forward passes are quite often tried at such a time. They are alright if the signaller has no confidence in the team's ability to gain by straight football or dependable trick play. But he should have tried at least two running plays before he resorts to the pass. Perhaps he can get it across in one or two rushing plays. If not, the pass stands as good a chance on the third or fourth down as it would if attempted on the first.

If you have on your team a fair drop or place kicker you should, as you begin to draw near to the opposing goal line, keep that man's ability in mind; and you should so maneuver your plays and team as to have the ball somewhere in front of the goal posts before the last down, so that on the last down, if you seem to have little or no chance of making your distance by another running play, you can at least try for a field goal with good chance of success.

## Summary.

1. Try end runs preferably on first or second downs.

2. Never order two end runs in succession.

3. Don't try an end run when the ball is less than 25 yards from your goal line, unless from punt formation.

4. Don't try an end run from close to the boundary.

5. If your end runs are being stopped look up and observe whether opponents haven't their line men all playing very wide, especially

the tackles. If they have you should buck continuously till you compel them to shorten up, when end runs may go again. The reverse rule will work just as well.

6. Try to divide up the work so you won't wear out any one player. But any man ought to be able to take the ball three times in succession at least, if there is reason for giving it to him successively.

7. When you find a weak spot you should persistently hammer that spot for the rest of the game. If you can't seem to put your finger on a weak spot in your enemy's line try to remember which of your backs seems to be gaining most ground and use him more than all the rest put together for the remainder of that game.

8. When a substitute comes into the game for opponents, send several hard plays at him immediately and find out just what he is good for.

9. Use bucks mainly when you need but a short gain.

10. Never forward pass inside your own 30-yard line.

11. The best down on which to forward pass is the third—the second is not bad.

12. If toward the end of third quarter you appear to be hopelessly beaten—because you have been unable to make headway with your running and bucking game—jump right into the

middle of a forward pass game. Let at least three plays out of four be passes. If they go wrong the score may mount up still higher against you, but as you are beaten anyway if you don't pull through by means of a passing game it makes small difference what the score mounts up to.

13. Put in a lot of practice even off the field, running over in your mind all your signals. Classify your plays so you can have all your end run numbers flash on the screen of your memory when your will calls for the end run list to present itself, and the same way with bucks, passes, tricks, etc.

14. Punt on first down if close to your own goal.

15. When in doubt punt anyway anywhere.

16. Don't give the ball to your punter for a hard run or buck on the play just before the one on which he likely will have to punt; his nerves will be too shaken and a poor punt will result.

17. Try not to get in the habit of calling a couple of plays only. If you have a fair variety of plays and your team executes them all well you should understand that variety of attack is a great asset to any team.

18. Call your signals in a snappy, cheery tone; the players will start and run in much the same way that you call signals.

19. If near either boundary on first or second down, and you wish to punt, you should pur-

posely spend a down in running the ball out of bounds so you may then bring it in 15 paces. From this position your punt will not be so apt to go out of bounds for only a few yards gain.

20.   Don't overlook the fact that a goal from the field will not do you any good if you are more than three points behind.  If there still remains a long time to play perhaps three points now will help if you think you can score additional points later on; but if there are but a few moments remaining to play, and three points would not win while six or seven would, you must stake everything on the chance of scoring a touchdown.

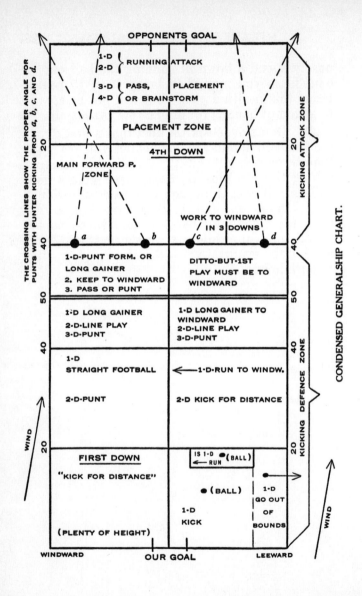

## CHAPTER XVI.

## GENERAL OBSERVATIONS ON
## FOOTBALL.

In a game involving bodily contact, as football, the big strong man has decided advantages. Other things being equal a good big man here must be better than a good little man.

But don't forget that other things are usually not equal. The smaller man is generally faster and nimbler, he has better use of himself, he co-ordinates better, he is often more aggressive than the bigger man, and he is frequently clearer headed and quicker witted. When, however, the big fellows have all these attributes in high degree and throw them into the game they become the really great players—the Hefflefingers, Hares, Hestons, De Witts, Coys and Thorpes.

\*　　\*　　\*　　\*　　\*

Considering the sum total of a player's natural qualifications for the game as represented by 100 per cent, the individual elements

—in the attainment of excellence—may be assigned the following valuations:

ATHLETIC TALENT (Acrobatic and gymnastic proclivity; love of sports; athletic instinct) .................. 25%

AGGRESSIVENESS (Courage, initiative, self-reliance, will power, stubborness, combativeness, ambition) .. 20%

MENTALITY (Ability to comprehend, to apprehend, to think rapidly, to keep cool, to remember, good perceptive faculties) .................... 20%

SPEED (In straight running, in nimbleness, shiftiness, dodging ability, etc.) ........................ 20%

WEIGHT (Strength, mass, power of impact, etc.) ..................... 15%

Total ..........................100%

\* \* \* \* \*

Granted a player possesses decided natural advantages, such as are found outlined in the above table, his success is then determined almost wholly by the kind of coaching and the kind of playing experience he gets—and they are, about, a 50-50 proposition.

Rating all-around natural qualifications, mental and physical, as constituting 50 per cent of the necessary ingredients entering into the final composition of a finished player, we may say that the other 50 per cent of excellence is due to his experience and his coaching —25 per cent each.

In no other game does high-grade coaching pay as big dividends in the development either of individual or team excellence as in the game of football.

\* \* \* \* \*

To the writer it seems that football may be boiled down into two great commandments. One of these relates to the Offense—"Thou shalt charge and block," while the other relates to the Defense—"Thou shalt charge and fight."

Clever plays are fine, blinding speed is excelcent, precision of play is admirable, rattlesnake tackling is great, sharp, hard blocking is splendid, smart headwork is indispensable and unyielding spirit is glorious in the game of football but; CHARGING—ah, there all adjectives fail me. Charging on the offense, charging on the defense, charging first, last and all the time, is the greatest thing in football.

\* \* \* \* \*

Ability to "follow the ball" is one of the greatest assets a player or a team can have. Whether on offense or on defense if you will follow the ball, will be near at hand, will be wherever the ball is you will generally be found to be playing good football. If snapshots of scrimmages always show you off to one side and never in the thick of things, depend upon it your coach will soon have you sitting on the bench.

So trail that ball like a bloodhound. You are tired? There's no such word in football. The other fellow is just as tired as you are—far more so if you have trained faithfully. Why? Because you have—you *must* have—better spirit than he, more "pep" and ambition than he, more courage, more stubbornness, more doggedness; because in a word, you're a better man than he; never admit even to yourself anything to the contrary. That's the mental and moral attitude of a real football player.

\*    \*    \*    \*    \*

The first duty of a soldier is to obey orders. It so happns it's the first duty of a football player as well.

The man that hesitates is lost. Even more surely the footballer that hesitates.

No one player or coach or team or college ever knew or will know all there is to know about football.

\*    \*    \*    \*    \*

A winning football team is never turned out by the coach and players alone. If there isn't the right football atmosphere in the entire college, if the whole sentiment of the institution isn't interestedly and loyally behind the football squad they will never win the championship no matter how much native talent they have nor how hard they work. It's spirit, in the last analysis, that wins in football, and much the greater part of that spirit must be infused into the squad by the rest of the college—the president, trustees, faculty, alumni, undergraduates, friends, and so on down even to the very janitors of the buildings.

When a team wins the coach gets twice as much credit as he deserves; when it loses he comes in for ten times as much blame as may justly be charged against him.

\* \* \* \* \*

Perhaps the greatest artificial trouble with which a coach has to contend is the exaggerated and wholly senseless praise that is showered upon even a fairly successful football player by press and public alike. It is the most harmful thing that can be done for the man. It takes a mighty level-headed and common-sense chap to keep from being spoiled by flattery of this character. He may have played ever so wonderful a game the year before, but let it be told to him too many times that he is a world's wonder on a football field and four times out of five that man's game starts going down hill. He gets to thinking and believing the coaches can no longer tell him anything about the game, forgetting they have followed it ofttimes more seasons than he has played games. Sometimes it takes bitter medicine to take this rottenness out of him again—it's like cutting out a cancer. And sometimes not even a major operation effects a cure; the man's spoiled for life.

But wonderful is the youth that can stand all this adulation and come through it all the same rollicking, unpuffed, ingenuous lad he was before the papers had ever heard of him or cared a snap of their fingers for his picture. All glory to him, and all friendship and good fellowship, too, for the remainder of his life. The game has made a great man of that chap.

## CHAPTER XVII.

## TREATMENT OF FOOTBALL INJURIES.

Even a short work on football would be unsatisfactory unless it devoted at least a few pages to the discussion of the commoner football injuries.

Of course, broken bones, dislocated joints, internal injuries and such serious pathological conditions are for the expert surgeon to handle. Happily these are not nearly so frequent in occurrence as prior to 1903, when the game underwent sweeping rule changes in order to make it safer.

But there are still a number of injuries bound to occur to every football team, and for many of these no physician or surgeon, as a rule, is greatly needed, because the injured player or his friends can usually handle his case by themselves with the aid of the advice and suggestions that follow:

### Sprains.

When you get a sprained joint you should stop playing immediately. It will recover three times as rapidly as it will if you continue to play upon it. Immediate rest is the very best thing.

The next thing is to get hot applications on the joint. It is better still if you can have a pail of water as hot as can possibly be borne and beside it a pail of very cold water. If the sprain is of the ankle stick the foot in the hot water two minutes, then take it out and plunge it into the cold water for one minute, then back into the hot for two, keeping up this alternation for 15 to 20 minutes.

If you use just the hot water alone dip towels in it and apply them to the sprain, changing the towels every minute, or as fast as they begin ever so little to cool off. When the fresh towel is laid on cover it at once with a dry towel so as to keep the steam in. Keep the hot water treatment up for 15 or 20 minutes. **Do not** rub the sprain with liniments or anything else—hot water, not liniment, is the first treatment for anything like a sprain or a muscle bruise or contusion, in which an acute inflammation is quickly generated. First of all you must get rid of this acute inflammation, and hot water is the best thing in the world for that.

Then stay off your feet. If it be a knee or ankle sprain get to your room and get in bed. Get an 8-ounce bottle of lead water and laudanum, of proper strength for burns and inflammations. Shake this up always before using, pour some out in a shallow dish like a saucer, shape up a layer of cotton to cover the sprained or bruised place, soak it in the lead water and then apply it just that way. Take care not to soil the bed linen with the lead water as the stain will not come out.

Every hour or oftener the cotton pad should be resoaked in the lead water and reapplied. The idea is to keep the injured place **wet** all the time with the lead water—no rubbing whatever. And this should be kept up all night long if possible.

In the morning another round of alternate hot and cold applications, then more lead water, at noon the same thing, and at night the same thing again, and so kept up until the heat and fever have left the joint.

Then we say the acute inflammation is gone and the joint or contusion is in a state of chronic inflammation. And now is the time to begin with liniments. Usually 24 hours of steady hot water and lead water applications will suffice to cool off the injured spot.

A first rate liniment for such injuries is made by mixing about three parts of soap liniment with one part of chloroform liniment and one-quarter of one part tincture of belladonna. Use it plentifully and it will make a fine lather that will greatly facilitate the rubbing.

A severe sprain should get at least two good rubs a day, and for several days the continued use of hot applications, two or three times a day, will stimulate circulation around the injury and will hasten its recovery.

When it has become well enough to bear some weight use a crutch or at least a cane for some days, and have it supported by a tight bandage. Then, when you go to playing again, always have it bandaged with adhesive tape before going out on the field and be careful, if it was an ankle, that your shoe is laced tightly all the way to the top. Elastic ankle supports are a good thing to wear for several seasons there-after. If the knee was ever sprained wear an elastic bandage there or else a rubber roller bandage every time you go out to play. The joint is and will be weak for a long time and it will need support for any strenuous work.

Sometimes a valuable player is so badly needed for a particular game close at hand that an effort must be made to have him in the game despite the sprain.

In such cases, if the sprain is not too serious, resort is had to strapping the injured joint very tightly with adhesive tape, at once, and leaving this on. It is all but impossible to describe without actual demonstration the different ways such strips should be applied in the case of different kinds of sprains, but the idea is to give external support to take the place of the lost internal support—the sprained ligament that has failed.

In no case should the adhesive be wrapped tightly around and around a sprained ankle or knee as that would completely cut off the circula-tion. The adhesive should be cut into strips long enough to go one-half or even three-fourths of the way around the injured joint but leaving an open, uncovered lane opposite the injured section through which lane blood can circulate.

## Cuts and Raw Places.

Liniments have nothing to do here; they would only make the cut or abrased surface smart like the mischief. They should be anti-septicised with iodine after first having been washed carefully with warm water. If the cut is deep it may best be treated by applying an ointment like unguentine. If not so deep but covering a considerable area, a good dusting powder like calomel will yield good results.

## Charley Horses.

This painful stiffness of the front thigh muscles is difficult to treat satisfactorily. There has been here a real tear of the muscle fibre and serum from the blood has oozed out of the tear and gone in between the fibres.

The serum then hardens, and so binds the fibres together that they lose their elasticity and cannot stretch without breaking away from the encircling hardened serum, and this calls for more tearing and so causes the severe pain each time the leg is raised.

Quick starts and fast running are to be avoided for some time in the treatment of "Charley Horses," but slow running and lots of walking are good for them. Apply hot cloths and afterwards give a good gripping massage—always running up toward the body, not down toward the feet. Also chop the thigh briskly with the edge of the hand to break the hardened serum up into small particles that can be carried away by the circulation.

It is claimed by some that to sleep with a cold, damp towel on it all night will effect a speedy cure. My own experience is that this does help sometimes but it is far from being an infallible remedy.

When you go out to work strap the front thigh muscles down tightly with broad adhesive strips stretched crosswise over the long muscles and reaching from the middle of the inside of the thigh to the middle of the outside of the thigh. This leaves the back of the thigh open for necessary blood circulation. A rubber roller bandage is often used here to good advantage.

**Enlarged ears** contain bruised blood that should be taken out. They should be lanced by a surgeon.

**Cuts** over the frontal bone of the eye nearly always require three or four stitches by a surgeon.

**Backaches** are helped by wearing porous plasters.

**Corn** plasters should be kept on hand for players who need them. No man can play a good game of ball if his feet are hurting him.

For **blisters** on the feet and for tender feet generally bathe them in salt water night and morning.

Some bruises on the bone are very slow to give up their painful sensation. They are often cured by a Cantharides (Spanish Fly) blister.

For general stiffness and soreness witch hazel or alcohol, or a mixture of the two, make a wholly satisfactory rubbing liniment.

After playing in a cold rain players, after taking their bath, should rub all over with alcohol saturated with raw quinine.

It is well to have a bottle of smelling salts handy.

An osteopath can do your cripples a lot of good in a great many refractory cases, and if you agree to send him all your men that need his treatment it is always possible to get them to make you a reasonable team rate.

Dry heat applied to bruised and contused places, water on the knee, etc., by means of electric bakers and pads, thermolites, etc., is very good indeed. If you have money with which to purchase such implements they should by all means be placed in the training house or dressing rooms. They are good for most any injury.

# CHAPTER XVIII.

## SUGGESTIONS TO THE COACH.

1.   On the field the Coach should be masterful and commanding, even dictatorial.  He should be short, sharp and decisive in his language. He has no time for "please" or "mister."

2.   He should not use profanity.  It is a great temptation, but it does no good.  It is not used in the class room, in the court room, nor in the clinic—why should it be used on the football field.  Cut it out and your players will turn out to be finer sportsmen and the faculty will support you better.

3.   If you make an obvious mistake frankly acknowledge it before the whole squad and take the blame.  Even coaches are human and commit errors.  Attempts to make your men believe otherwise will only result in the loss of their respect for you.  You will soon find them promptly shouldering the blame for their own faults and short comings if you set the example which will make for harmony and good feeling among the team members, besides enabling you the more quickly to locate the trouble.

4.   It is not enough to tell a player that he has failed in a given duty; generally he knows that much himself.  You should be able to tell him **how** he failed and to explain to him **why** he failed.

5.   If a play that looked good on paper doesn't seem to work out to advantage in scrimmage don't be too quick to "scrap" it.  Perhaps some one player merely failed in the performance of his unit duty.  Try to find whether any player is "gumming it up."  This will require perceptive faculties; cultivate them.

6.   Off the field a coach should never be curt but always kindly, affable, genial and approachable in the extreme.  He should mix with them socially, but no more or less, than do most members of the faculty with their students.  The players should be encouraged to come to him freely with their questions and problems.  Even their ideas and suggestions should be invited and listened to with attention and answered without ridicule no matter how absurd or preposterous they may be.  This will make the players feel they are integral parts of the machine and the responsibility will make men of them.

7.   It's a good plan to send the entire squad to the blackboard once or twice a week.  Group the halves together, the ends together, etc.  Have them alternate in diagraming and explaining to each other every play you have given them.  If any difference of opinion arises as to the duty

of the player in a given group on a certain play you can set right all the players in that group by one correcting statement.

8.   The coach should permit no back-talk from any player, not even from the captain.  He will get none if he carries himself with dignity, though he must at times be severe, arbitrary and little short of a Czar.  He must never be abusive in his language.

9.   The coach must be absolutely impartial at all times.  Like every other human being he probably likes some of his players better than others, but he must never show this to his squad. They will work much harder if they feel they are getting a square deal and that the places go without fail to the best men, regardless of any other consideration.

10.   Never let players squabble or quarrel or fight even in practice scrimmages.  Tell them to save all that for the enemy.  It is best not even to permit them to indulge in useless talking. Instead, they should keep silent and listen to the coaching, and that way the coach will be able to make his instructions heard without the need of exasperating repetition.

There should be as good order and as business-like an air about all football practice as there is in a first class bank or on a military drill ground.

11.   While a coach should not spare the whip lashing of a keen tongue whenever a reprimand

or a rebuke has been merited, he should be equally quick to give deserved and open praise to any and every man for any fine play, or even for a good effort. Neither praise nor blame alone will ever bring out a man's best through prolonged periods.

12. A coach should be careful not to call on players to do things that are well nigh humanly impossible, and he should not overlook that what may have been possible for some one player is by no means possible to all players. He should study their capabilities and their limitations and design his plays and system in accordance. The plays that went well with last year's team may be wholly unsuited to this year's Eleven. Cut your cloth according to your man.

13. Keep your men encouraged but never let them get "cocky." When signs of overconfidence appear find a way to take it out of them before the game comes along. But, on the whole, it is better to keep them in a cheerful, optimistic frame of mind than in a state of pessimism and depression. Give them the alternate hot and cold water treatment—first blow hot, then blow cold. The team never lived that didn't need it just that way.

14. It's a good idea, occasionally, to call for three questions from every man on the squad, concerning points of play, formations, signals, rules or what not that he does not understand. As a rule they are too diffident to ask such questions before the others, fearing to expose their

ignorance. They should be asked to sign their names to the papers, but assurance should be given them that in discussing and answering the questions in the presence of the entire squad their names will not be divulged. Never laugh at any such questions no matter how ridiculous they may be. You will be much surprised to find what excellent questions are often asked and also, on the other hand, to learn what very simple things puzzle them, things you would not have thought at all necessary to explain.

15. If you have no assistant coaches that can be spared to work out with novices or late arrivals, appoint one of your smartest players to take these men in hand. Injured players who cannot get into real action, yet want to do something to help, make excellent coaches to green men, provided of course you are sure they know the system themselves. This not only leaves you free to attend to other duties, but the schooling the improvised player-coach gets out of his own earnest efforts to explain the formation, plays, signals, etc., to some other player crystallizes his own knowledge of the subject and helps him immeasurably. And perhaps the new man can understand his fellow player better than he can you; at all events he feels more at home with him.

16. Never be late getting out on the field; both coach and captain should always set good examples. If you take the whole squad, or only

some of the men, to a different part of the field for special instruction always take them on the run. Allow no slow walking about a field by anybody in uniform. A football field is a place for running, not walking.

17. In signal drill I stop the whole team instantly if but one man is at fault in performing his duty on that particular play, and I correct the error then and there. But if the error occurred in scrimmage it is best not to lose the valuable playing time of 21 other men while correcting the mistake of one; wait till there is a lull in the playing, then have it out with the delinquent.

18. If a player makes a palpably poor play, a silly error, or constantly forgets the simplest things I penalize him for it by imposing some penalty equally silly or by making him go over the thing by himself many times. For instance:

If he fails to fall on a live ball lying loose upon the ground—even if the work in hand is only passing the ball rapidly in a circle, or in signal drill, I have a standing penalty of falling on it 10 times over in a corner alone.

When I call "All up!" it means everybody come up to where I am **on the run.** If they fail to come on the run they can try running all the way around the track by themselves.

If a player drops or fumbles a ball through sheer carelessness I give him one to take to the fence and there bounce it against the fence 100 times, catching it each time it rebounds and putting it under his arm in proper carrying position.

Penalties such as these cure men of persistent faults much more quickly than any amount of scolding.

| 1935 | Jay Berwanger | Chicago |
| 1936 | Larry Kelley | Yale |
| 1937 | Clint Frank | Yale |
| 1938 | Davey O'Brien | Texas Christian |
| 1939 | Nile Kinnick | Iowa |
| 1940 | Tom Harmon | Michigan |
| 1941 | Bruce Smith | Minnesota |
| 1942 | Frank Sinkwich | Georgia |
| 1943 | Angelo Bertelli | Notre Dame |
| 1944 | Les Horvath | Ohio State |
| 1945 | Felix Blanchard | Army |
| 1946 | Glenn Davis | Army |
| 1947 | John Lujack | Notre Dame |
| 1948 | Doak Walker | Southern Methodist |
| 1949 | Leon Hart | Notre Dame |
| 1950 | Vic Janowicz | Ohio State |
| 1951 | Dick Kazmaier | Princeton |
| 1952 | Billy Vessels | Oklahoma |
| 1953 | John Lattner | Notre Dame |
| 1954 | Alan Ameche | Wisconsin |
| 1955 | Howard Cassady | Ohio State |
| 1956 | Paul Hornung | Notre Dame |
| 1957 | John Crow | Texas A&M |
| 1958 | Peter Dawkins | Army |
| 1959 | Billy Cannon | Louisiana State |
| 1960 | Joe Bellino | Navy |
| 1961 | Ernie Davis | Syracuse |
| 1962 | Terry Baker | Oregon State |
| 1963 | Roger Staubach | Navy |
| 1964 | John Huarte | Notre Dame |

| 1965 | Mike Garrett | Southern California |
| 1966 | Steve Spurrier | Florida |
| 1967 | Gary Beban | UCLA |
| 1968 | O. J. Simpson | Southern California |
| 1969 | Steve Owens | Oklahoma |
| 1970 | Jim Plunkett | Stanford |
| 1971 | Pat Sullivan | Auburn |
| 1972 | Johnny Rodgers | Nebraska |
| 1973 | John Cappalletti | Penn State |
| 1974 | Archie Griffin | Ohio State |
| 1975 | Archie Griffin | Ohio State |
| 1976 | Tony Dorsett | Pittsburgh |
| 1977 | Earl Campbell | Texas |
| 1978 | Billy Sims | Oklahoma |
| 1979 | Charles White | Southern California |
| 1980 | George Rogers | South Carolina |
| 1981 | Marcus Allen | Southern California |
| 1982 | Herschel Walker | Georgia |
| 1983 | Mike Rosier | Nebraska |
| 1984 | Doug Fluttie | Boston College |
| 1985 | Bo Jackson | Auburn |
| 1986 | Vinny Testaverde | Miami |
| 1987 | Tim Brown | Norte Dame |
| 1988 | Barry Sanders | Oklahoma State |
| 1989 | Andre Ware | Houston |
| 1990 | Ty Detmer | Brigham Young |
| 1991 | Demond Howard | Michigan |
| 1992 | Gino Torretta | Miami |
| 1993 | Charlie Ward | Florida State |
| 1994 | Rashaan Salaam | Colorado |

| | | |
|---|---|---|
| 1995 | Eddie George | Ohio State |
| 1996 | Danny Wuerffel | Florida |
| 1997 | Charles Woodson | Michigan |
| 1998 | Ricky Williams | Texas |
| 1999 | Ron Dayne | Wisconsin |